Vintage Aircraft
Nose Art

Gary M. Valant

Motorbooks International
Publishers & Wholesalers ®

First published in 1987 by Motorbooks International
Publishers & Wholesalers Inc, PO Box 2, 729 Prospect
Avenue, Osceola, WI 54020 USA

Printed in China

The information in this book is true and complete to
the best of our knowledge. All recommendations are
made without any guarantee on the part of the author or
publisher, who also disclaim any liability incurred in
connection with the use of this data or specific details

Library of Congress Cataloging-in-Publication Data
Valant, Gary.
    Vintage aircraft nose art.

    1. Airplanes, Military—Decoration.   2. Airplanes,
Military—Decoration—Pictorial works.   I. Title.
UG1240.V35   1987   358.4'183   87-20360
ISBN 0-87938-266-X

Contents

Dedication

This book is dedicated to all of the air crews whose humor and imagination decorated World War II combat aircraft, and to those who strive to preserve the great history and aircraft of that era.

My special thanks to the following people.

Clarence Simonsen of Alberta, Canada, who supplied many of the very hard to find color photos and related information. Clarence has been interested in aircraft for as long as he can remember, and has been collecting nose art since the 1960s. He has written many articles and has had a nose art column in the *Eighth Air Force News*.

Paul M. Andrews of Vienna, Virginia, has been invaluable in the identification of the Eighth Air Force nose art. He is currently working on a compilation of the combat missions of the 95th Bomb Group that will be incorporated into their unit history, and has also written a number of articles about the Eighth Air Force.

Robert Mann for his assistance on the 19th and 98th Bomb Group B-29s.

Antony Giacobbe for his nose art files and contacts.

Tim Bivens for all of his contributions.

Leland "Pappy" Martin of the Confederate Air Force, along with Tony and Javier, who spent the night moving all of that equipment around the hangar while I photographed the nose art hanging on the walls.

Melissa Keiser of the National Air and Space Museum for all of her assistance before and during our visit.

The fine staff at the US Air Force Museum, Dayton, Ohio.

Everyone else who sent information or photographs in support of this book.

The crew and unit commander of USAF F-111 "Lucky Strike," whose nose art got me interested in doing this book.

And last, but not least, my family: Nancy, Bonnie and Michael, who gave me so much help and support on this project.

Preface

It's mid-winter 1943, you're twenty years old, it's 04:30 in the morning, it's raining, it's cold. You've got a slight hangover, and you're walking in mud (there's always mud).

You're wearing a fur-lined flying suit, because where you're going it's thirty degrees below zero. You've got an oxygen mask, because where you're going it's hard to breathe. You're carrying a map, because at 25,000 feet there are no signs. Prior to December 7, 1941, your main goal in life was to get a car and marry Ginger Rogers, but now it's just to stay alive another day, because you're a crewman on a B-17, and where you're going, people are going to die.

But not *you*, not *your* plane, not *your* crew, because you're special, and the special people always come back. They don't blow up in the sky, or go in at 400 miles per hour, one wing gone, no chutes, on fire—not the special ones; they always come back.

So we need a special name for our plane—and a special picture on it. Maybe a picture of Betty Grable, or one of those Vargas girls from *Esquire.* And we'll name it something like "Sack Time," "Mister Completely" or "Target For Tonight." But it has to be special, and when it's finished, it will be ready—
Ready for Duty.

Introduction

It was good or it was bad, it was naughty or nice, funny or sad, and sometimes it was self-deprecating, and during World War II it was everywhere. It has come to be known as *nose art*, because it was normally found on or about the nose of the aircraft.

The origin of nose art goes back to some ancient time when the first proud charioteer decorated his vehicle so that it would be distinguishable from the others. The desire to personalize an object, a machine, to make it unique among the multitude, is basic to man's nature. Place man under great stresses, give him a very uncertain future, and this desire can become an obsession. So it is in war, and with the machines of war. A thousand B-17s, identical in every way, roll off the assembly line and fly to an uncertain fate, but each one can be different. The difference is not in the tail number. Those are for record keepers and ribbon clerks. The difference is in the imagination and talent of the crew. Few crew members would talk about 247613 or 34356, but many tales would be told about "Sack Time" or "The Dragon Lady."

The ideas for nose art came from everywhere; girlfriends, wives, posters, matchbook covers, calendars, the comics or some event related to the history of the aircraft. The "Swamp Angel" landed in a swamp, "Patched Up Piece" had probably been repaired more than once. "Just Once More" seems like a reasonable request for a B-17 crew trying to complete twenty-five missions so they could go home. "Better

Duck" could have two meanings, and "SHEDONWANNA?" could relate to problems that the crew had with the aircraft.

But the majority of the nose art was inspired by the artwork in the magazines and calendars of the time. Disney characters were prevalent, as well as the comic strips such as Al Capp's "L'il Abner," or Milton Caniff's "Terry and the Pirates." But the most widely copied artist was Alberto Vargas.

B-17 Waist gunner in action. *NASM*

Vargas was the premier pin-up artist of our time. Everyone has seen his work, whether it was a pin-up, a movie poster or a perfume ad. During the war, Vargas was the main artist for *Esquire* magazine, producing most of the artwork for the magazine's pin-up page and calendars. I think it would be safe to say that the arrival of a new *Esquire* with one of Vargas' exquisite airbrushed artworks was a red-letter day around the world.

The artwork could be painted on the plane by anyone. Those units fortunate enough to have talented artists produced excellent nose art. Some units went so far as to recruit artists, while some did without. It all had to do with the place, the people and the situation. Some of the remote outfits did not have the paint to do detailed work, while others had all they could ask for. So nose art came in all different shapes and sizes. The small ones could fit on a card table, while some of the B-29 artwork was bigger than a billboard.

There is no question that the golden age of nose art was during World War II and Korea. World War II was a time during which almost anything was allowed in an effort to boost morale and unit efficiency. But, as is the case with most things, a free hand led to some excesses and some censorship is evident in some of the artwork. After Korea, nose art all but disappeared from US aircraft. Artwork reappeared on a few Vietnam-vintage planes, but then it disappeared again. I am happy to report that nose art is making a comeback, slowly but surely, as commanders begin to see the positive effects that it has on air crews and their support personnel. Nose art can be beautiful, inspiring and in good taste.

—Sgt. Arnold Thurm

Cartoon from "Yank"—How nose art is really painted. . .

CAF collection

The Confederate Air Force in Harlingen, Texas, has perhaps the largest collection of authentic World War II nose art in the world. These are all panels that were cut off of aircraft being scrapped at Walnut Ridge, Arkansas, in 1946.

Although there is more than one version of this story, the most accurate one seems to be as follows: After the war, Brown and Root had a salvage operation at Walnut Ridge, where they scrapped out salvage aircraft for the aluminum under the name of Aircraft Conversion Company. The overall operation was so large, that at one time after World War II they owned more combat aircraft than the US government. This would have made them the first or second largest air force in the world.

Minot Pratt, general manager of the company, took a fancy to the nose art panels, and had a workman remove the "interesting" nose art with a fire axe. It seems that his idea was to build a fence around his property out of nose art. This never came to pass, so the panels were stored in the barn, and were later moved to west Texas when Pratt started a cattle company. The panels were given to the CAF in the mid-1960s. Regardless of the whys and wherefores, we are all in debt to this man for saving a piece of history. I would rather have the panels to look at than to fry eggs in.

Caption key

The following example will help you decipher the system I have used to identify each photograph.

Night Mission B-24-D 44-40891 234 BS 567 BG 47 AF Lost April 16, 1944. CAF/G. *Valant*

Night Mission is the nose art name
B-24-D is the aircraft type
44-40891 is the aircraft serial number
234 BS 567 BG 47 AF is the unit assignment
Lost April 16, 1944. is additional information about the aircraft
CAF/G. *Valant* is the source of the photograph for artifact/photographer

Source key

AFM stands for US Air Force Museum, Dayton, Ohio
NASM stands for National Air and Space Museum, Washington, DC
CAF stands for Confederate Air Force, Harlingen, Texas

Double Trouble as first painted. Two props. *H. Russell*

Sloppy But Safe on R&R AFM

Easy Maid stands on Iwo Jima, August 1945. *John Gardner*

Surprise Attack AFM

Mama Foo Foo *Clarence Ligocki*

Nobby's Harriet J B-17 The last photo of this aircraft before being scrapped at Walnut Ridge, AR, in 1946. *J. Wisler*

Brinkman nose art

Before the war, Mr. Brinkman was an advertising artist in the Chicago and St. Louis area. By the time he was drafted into the Army Air Corps he had six years experience as a commercial artist. There were no openings in special services for his talents, so he was assigned to a Guard unit at Davis-Monthan Army Air Base, Tucson, Arizona. Along with his other duties, he began to do art work and mess hall murals in the base area.

At this time of the war, November 1943, the 486th Bomb Group had just moved to Davis-Monthan for training. When the commander of the 834th Bomb Squadron, Capt W. D. Howell, saw some of Brinkman's work, he offered Brinkman a chance to transfer to the 834th. There and then, a nose art idea was born. Why not decorate each of the twelve B-24s in the 834th with a sign of the Zodiac?

Early in April 1944, the 486th arrived at station 174, Sudbury, Suffolk, England, and Brinkman began painting the nose art on the B-24s. In total, Brinkman painted twelve Zodiacs, but you will find two Leos and no Taurus. In Brinkman's own words, "As I recall, the missing Zodiac was Taurus the Bull. All I remember was I started this sign three times and on the different B-24s, then they would take off and never return." As there are no records of any B-24 aircraft losses in the 834th, we can assume that the aircraft were transferred to other units.

The following photos are of Brinkman's sketches and finished work.

Varga Girls

The following photographs are of some of the artwork of Alberto Vargas, which appeared in *Esquire* magazine during World War II. Interestingly, during this period Vargas painted under the name Varga—hence the name of this group of paintings, Varga Girls. *Esquire* holds the copyright on this artwork: Varga Girls copyright © (years of original publication) 1987 Esquire Assoc. Note the attempt to faithfully reproduce the drawing as closely as possible in most cases.

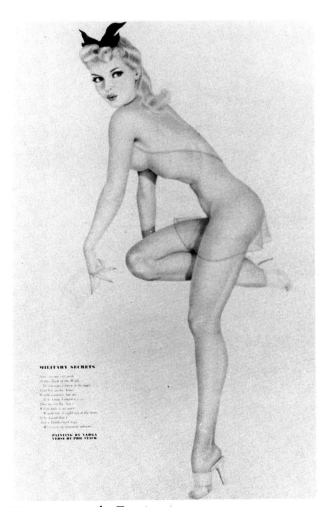

Vargas artwork. *Esquire.*

Target for Tonight B-24 *Esquire.* AFM

B-24 *Esquire.*

Mission Belle B-24-D 42-40389 400 BS Aircraft lost over Rabul November 18, 1943. *Esquire.* AFM

The Dark Angel B-26 *Esquire.* AFM

Scrumptious B-26 *Esquire.* AFM

"Over Exposed" *Esquire.* AFM

Miss Gee Eyewanta (Go Home) B-17 401
BG 8 AF *Esquire.* NASM

Other pin-ups were frequently used over
and over throughout the world. The following
was one of the more popular.

Wheel n Deal B-29 *Esquire.* AFM

Miss 'B' Haven B-17 42-31863 401 BG 8AF Began service
February 6, 1944; salvaged February 19, 1945. *Esquire.* NASM

Jamaica? B-24-H 41-28746 785 BS 466 BG *Esquire.* NASM

Taylor Maid B-24-J 44-41204 308 BG *Esquire.* AFM

:Our Gal: B-24 *Esquire. NASM*

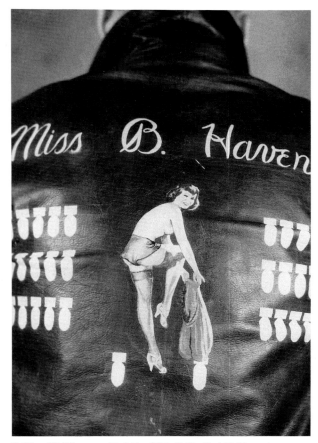

Miss B Haven B-17 401 BG 8 AF *Esquire.
NASM*

B-26 42-107625 *Esquire. AFM*

Little Pink Panties B-26-C 42-107841
Esquire. AFM

Vargas artwork. *Esquire.*

5 Grand B-17 43-37716 96 8 AF AFM

Dream Girl in service in Korea. *NASM*

Lucky Strike B-24 *NASM*

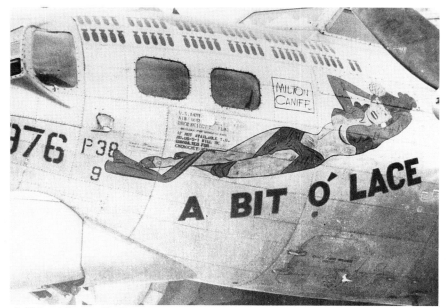

A Bit o' Lace *C. Simonsen*

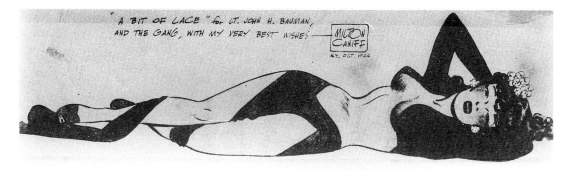

The original sketch by Caniff for **A Bit o' Lace.** *C. Simonsen*

The cartoon with Miss Lace as seen in the army camp newspapers. *C. Simonsen*

23

The Shack *C. Simonsen*

The Moose is Loose Contemporary USAF nose art. *J. Adderly*

Temptation B-17 42-30188 96 BG 8AF Salvaged Feburary 4, 1944. *AFM*

Old Irongut B-17 *NASM*

Shack Rabbit B-17 42-3318 96 BG 8 AF Lost on a mission to Kerlin/Bastard on September 23, 1945. *NASM*

Sugar Puss B-17 42-3088 94 BG 8 AF *AFM*

24

Frenesi B-17 Pronounced "Free n Easy," this 8th AF B-17 piloted by Lt. Cely is shown after a large raid—"just a series of holes held together by some metal"—with three wounded gunners. *AFM*

Shoo Shoo Baby B-17 42-31669 303BG 8 AF Lost April 24, 1944, over Landsberg. *NASM*

Patches n' Prayers B-17 42-37733 381 BG 8 AF Began service February 22, 1944; Lost April 18, 1944. *NASM*

Mary Cary B-17 42-97405 360 BS 303BG 8AF Began service April 30, 1944; lost June 22, 1944. *NASM*

Sunkist Special B-17 91 BG 8AF *Andrews AFB*

Oops—what happened to the "Kist?" *NASM*

Jacket patch and map from the China-Burma-India (CBI) Theater.

Miss Bea Havin B-17 NASM

The Black Swan B-17 42-29895 324BSQ 91BG 8AF NASM

Scrappy Jr B17 44-83264 452 BG 8AF NASM

Screwball Express B-17 42-97128 379 BG 8AF Began service March 23, 1944; lost April 5, 1945. NASM

Yankee Belle B-17-G 42-32085 91 BG 8AF Began service July 10, 1944; Lost on a mission to Berlin February 3, 1945. NASM

Lightning Strikes B-17 42-3073 563BS 388BG 8AF NASM

Idaliza B-17 42-97546 303BG 8AF Began service March 12, 1944; declared beyond repair January 30, 1945. NASM

Ack-Ack Annie B-17 42-32095 95 BG 8AF Began service March 16, 1944; survived the war. NASM

Alley-Oop B-17 42-5854 303BG 8AF Began service with 303DR on July 13, 1943, returned to US April 15, 1944. NASM

Baby Lu B-17 42-106992 401 BG 8AF NASM

Belle of the Blue B-17 42-30094 385 BG 8AF NASM

Colonel Bub B-17 381BG NASM

Daddy's Delight B-17-G 42-97422 303BG 8AF Began service June 2, 1944; salvaged April 7, 1945. NASM

Dame Satan B-17 322BS 91BG 8AF Lost on a mission to Schweinfurt, August 17, 1943. NASM

Dame Satan II B-17 42-31070 322BS 91BG 8AF Returned to the US June 18, 1944. NASM

Delta Rebel B-17 91BG 322BS 8AF AFM

Delta Rebel No2 B-17 42-5077 Clark Gable, a B-17 waist gunner in the 8AF admires **Delta Rebel No2** 91BG 322BS 8AF lost August 12, 1942, on a mission to Gelsenkirchen. AFM

Demo Darling B-17 42-39774 323BS 91BG 8AF NASM

Desperate Journey B-17 42-3053 Maj. Aycock stands beside B-17 at the 324BS 91BG 8AF. NASM

Dog Breath B-17-G 42-31330 401BG NASM

Better Do'er! B-17 44-6977 303BG 8AF Began service February 1, 1945; survived the war. NASM

Doris-Jr B-17 NASM

Dottie B-17 92BG 8AF NASM

The Duchess (Sure Stuff)! B-17 8AF NASM

Duke of Paducah B-17 401BS 91BG 8AF The bent nose is from a mid-air collision with **Black Swan.** AFM

Duchess' Daughter B-17G-45-80 42-97272 303BG 8AF Joined the 303 on April 19, 1944. NASM

Wreck of *Duchess' Daughter* after wheels-up landing July 1944. Note all four engines were off before landing. NASM

Dynamite John B-17 401BG 8AF NASM

Eager Beaver B-17 793BS India. NASM

The Eagle's Wrath B-17 91BG Lost August 17, 1943, on a mission to Schweinfurt. *NASM*

El Lobo B-17 42-24593 305 BG 8AF Lost February 4, 1943, over Emdem. Flash suppressors on 50-cal. machine guns. *NASM*

Equipoise B-17 42-30580 92BG *NASM*

E-Rat-Icator B-17G-10-VE 42-38970 452BG 8AF Note flack hole repair panels. Bomb is labeled "rat poison." *NASM*

Exterminator B-17 92BG 8AF *NASM*

Extra Special B-17 322BS 91BG 8AF *NASM*

Fancy Nancy IV B-17 42-31662 401BG 8AF Salvaged April 25, 1945. *NASM*

FDR's Potato Peeler Kids B-17 42-5243 303BG *NASM*

Fearless Fosdick B-17G-GQ-BO #42-102957 358BS 303BG 8AF *NASM*

Fickle Finger of Fate B-17 42-3335 385 BG 8AF Salvaged April 9, 1945. *NASM*

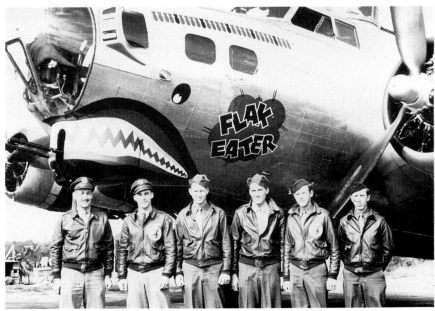

Flak Eater B-17 44-6009 305BG 8AF Began service April 17, 1944; survived the war. *NASM*

Flak Flirter B-17G 43-38366 493 BG 8AF Salvaged April 15, 1945 *NASM*

Flak-Shy Lady B-17 43-39326 452BG NASM

Flyin' Hobo B-17 381BG NASM

Flying Jenny B-17 525BS 379BG 8AF NASM

Forget Me Not II B-17 381BG 8AF NASM

Fort Alamo II B-17F-B5-HO #42-29896 Italy. NASM

Fort Worth Gal B-17G-40-DL 44-6095 381BG NASM

Hell's Halo B-17 322BS 91BG 8AF NASM

Hell Zapoppin B-17 92BG 8AF NASM

Henn's Revenge B-17 44-8427 303BG 8 AF Began service
October 23, 1943; declared beyond repair April 10, 1945. NASM

Hey Daddy B-1743-8036 91BG 8AF NASM

Hi-Doc! B-17 NASM

Hit Parade Jr B-17 385 BG 8AF NASM

Holy Mackeral! B-17 41-42609 303BG 8AF Began service October 24, 1942; lost over Paris April 4, 1943. *NASM*

Hustlin' Hussy B-17 42-30354 385 BG 8AF Lost on a mission to Frankfurt January 29, 1944. *Andrews AFB*

Incendiary Blonde B-17 44-6951 91 BG 8AF Began service November 4, 1944; survived the war. *NASM*

Ice Cold Katy B-17 401BG 8AF *NASM*

Ice Col' Katy B-17 381 BG 8AF *NASM*

Jack the Ripper B-17 41-24490 324BS 91BG Lost February 22, 1944. *NASM*

Jap-Happy B-17E #41-2520 NASM

Jezebel B-17 91BG 8AF NASM

The Joker B-17F 42-29888 NASM

Kipling's Error the III B-17 42-5885 96BG 8AF Lost on a mission to Rostock April 11, 1944. NASM

The Klap-Trap II 42-30130 96BG 8AF Lost over Ludwigshafen, January 7, 1944. B-17

Knock-Out Dropper B-17 41-24605 359BS 303BG 8AF NASM

Lady Satan B-17 42-97175 452 BG 8AF Lost February 6, 1945. *NASM*

Lewd Angel B-17G-95-BO 43-38755 91BG 8AF *NASM*

Liberty Belle B-17F 42-30096 544BS 385 BG 8AF *NASM*

Little Pedro B-17 43-37736 401BG 8AF Began service June 10, 1944; salvaged November 8, 1944. *NASM*

Little Tush B-17 42-102595 303BS 8AF Began service June 6, 1944 (D-Day); salvaged August 8, 1944. *NASM*

Los Lobos B-17 *NASM*

Madame Shoo Shoo B-17G 43-37707 322BS 91BG 8AF Began service June 28, 1944; beyond repair April 8, 1945. *NASM*

Madame Queen B-17 42-97931 401BG 8AF Began service June 1, 1944; survived the war. *NASM*

Margie Mae B-17 42-5847 381BG 8AF Lost on a mission to Gelsenkirchen August 12, 1943. *NASM*

Meat Hound B-17 42-29524 303 BG 8AF Began service July 30, 1943; lost over Oschersleben January 11, 1944. *NASM*

Mis-Abortion B-17 381BG This name offended someone, and was later changed to "Stuff." *NASM*

Stuff B-17 42-2371 *NASM*

Miss Umbriago B-1742-97187 360 BS 303BG 8AF Began service March 26, 1944; lost on a mission to Magdeburg, September 28, 1944. *NASM*

Mollita B-17 43-37817 452 BG 8AF Salvaged July 14, 1944. *NASM*

The Mustang (Buck Shot) B-17F *NASM*

Miss Dee-Day B-17 8AF 305BF Could mean Miss D-Day (invasion) or misty day—common in England. *NASM*

Maggie B-17 42-31091 401BG 8AF Began service November 11, 1943; lost September 11, 1944. *NASM*

Manchester Misses B-17G 452BG #44-8799 *NASM*

43

Margie B-17 43-38379 323BS 91BG 8AF NASM

Mary Lou B-17 42-97504 323BS 91BG 8AF Salvaged October 14, 1944. NASM

Minnie the Mermaid B-17 42-31614 381BG 8AF Began service January 21, 1944; lost February 22, 1944. NASM

Miss Lace B-17 42-102411 303BG 8AF Began service April 30, 1944; salvaged March 28, 1945. NASM

Not To-Day Cleo B-17G-100-80 43-38917 452BG 8AF NASM

Now Go! B-17 42-97780 452BG 8AF Began service April 28, 1944; survived the war. NASM

Old Bill B-17 42-29673 8AF Began service April 6, 1943; salvaged April 16, 1943. *NASM*

Ol' Mac B-17 305BG 8AF *NASM*

Old Coffins B-17 42-30018 381BG 8AF Salvaged March 20, 1944. *NASM*

Ole Swayback B-17 381BG *NASM*

Oh Happy Day B-17C-95-BO 43-38790 *NASM*

Ooold Soljer B-17 41-24559 303BG 360BS 8AF Began service October 24, 1942; salvaged April 1, 1943. *NASM*

Our Boarding House B-17 381BG NASM

Pakawalup B-17 42-97630 457BG 8AF NASM

Patty Jo B-17 42-31242 563BS 388BG 8AF NASM

Peace or Bust B-17 91BG 8AF NASM

Pella Tulip B-17G 42-102703 381BG Began service April 22, 1944; salvaged October 14, 1944. NASM

Pistol Packin' Mama B-17 42-30791 305BG 8AF NASM

Pregnant Portia B-17 42-30263 385BG 8AF Salvaged November 2, 1943. NASM

Pride of the "Kiarians" B-17 Undergoes major repairs. NASM

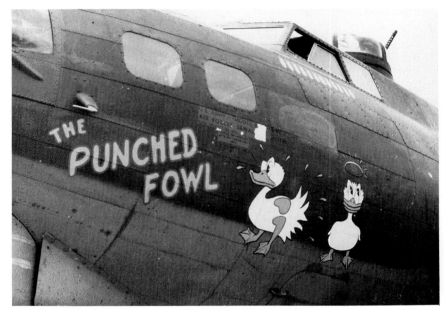

The Punched Fowl B-17 452 BG 730 BS 8AF NASM

Ramp Rooster B-17 42-107188 398BG 8AF Began service May 5, 1944; lost December 29, 1944. NASM

Rat poison Tail art on rear gunner area. B-17 NASM

Redmond Annie B-17 Annie is riding a mule and has a B-17 on a string. NASM

Rough-Neck B-17 North Africa. NASM

Roxy's Special B-17 43-38348 322BS 91BG 8AF Began service August 18, 1944; lost on a mission to Ludwigshafen September 8, 1944. NASM

Rusty Dusty B-17 44-6578 322BS 91BG 8AF Began service December 7, 1944; salvaged April 4, 1945. NASM

Sack Time B-17 42-102544 303BG 8AF Began service April 12, 1944; lost over Dresden April 17, 1945. NASM

"Sack Time" B-17 42-5912 385 BG 8AF Lost to Regensburg August 17, 1943. Note bucket on prop spinner. NASM

The Saint & Ten Sinners B-17 401BG NASM

Scorchy II B-17 42-97058 359BS 303BG 8AF Began March 27, 1944; lost over Aschaffenburg January 21, 1945. *NASM*

Screamin' Red Ass B-17 42-30340 388BG 563 BS 8AF Lost March 8, 1944, on a mission to Berlin. *NASM*

Screw B-17 *NASM*

Shack Bunny B-17 42-5914 385 BG 8AF *NASM*

Shangi-La Lil B-17 42-29754 303BG 360BS 8AF Began service June 17, 1943; lost over Watten August 27, 1943. *NASM*

She's A Honey B-17-G 43-38970 305BG 8 AF *NASM*

Shoo Shoo Baby B-17 42-97311 303 BG 8AF Began service April 13, 1944; survived the war. *NASM*

Shoo-Shoo Baby B-24 *AFM*

Slightly Dangerous B-17 42-3293 388 BG 563 BS 8 AF Lost to Stuttgart September 6, 1943, on nineteenth mission. Caught fire after a fighter attack; five crewman survived. *NASM*

Smashing Time B-17 43-38158 381BG 8 AF Salvaged January 21, 1945. *NASM*

Spare Parts B-17 305 BG 8 AF *NASM*

Sparky B-17 44-8125 360BS 303 BG 8 AF *NASM*

Special Delivery B-17-G 42-102496 359 BS 303 BG 8 AF
Began April 30, 1944; crashed September 18, 1944. *NASM*

Stag Party B-17-G 43-37837 305 BG 8 AF *NASM*

Star Dust B-17 43-38901 322 BS 91 BG 8AF *NASM*

Stars and Stripes B-17 42-3544 385 BG 8AF Lost January 5,
1944, on a mission to Bordeaux. *NASM*

Stinky B-17 322 BS 91 BG 8 AF *NASM*

Stric Nine B-17 42-29475 91 BG 323BS 8AF Began service
March 7, 1943; lost on a mission to Caen July 10, 1943. *NASM*

51

Swamp Fire B-17 42-32024 525 BS 379 BG 8 AF 100th mission marker. The aircraft survived the war. NASM

Sweet Dish B-17 44-6586 91 BG 8 AF NASM

Texas Chubby-The J'Ville Jolter B-17 42-31634 8 AF Lost August 16, 1944. NASM

Target for Tonite B-17 41-24615 305BG 8 AF NASM

Tempest Turner B-17 43-38216 493BG 8 AF NASM

Tiger Girl B-17 388BG 560BS 8 AF NASM

To Tokyo B-17 NASM

Toots B-17 42-29606 303BG 8AF Began service April 6, 1943; lost on a mission to Hamburg July 25, 1943. NASM

Touch the Button Nell II B-17 42-38117 381 BG 8AF Began service February 26, 1944; lost July 4, 1944. NASM

Tower of London B-17 91BG 8AF NASM

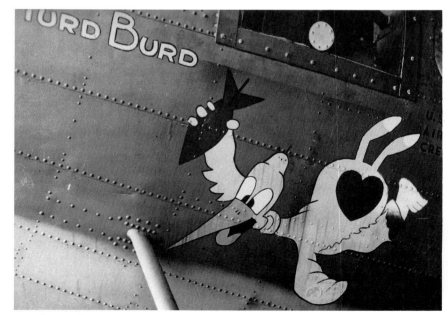

Turd Burd B-17 305 BG 8AF NASM

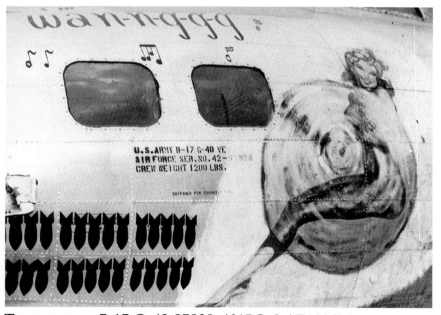

Twan-n-g-g-g B-17-G 42-97838 401BG 8 AF NASM

Uncle Sammy B-17 381 BG NASM

Under Ground Farmer B-17-G 44-6020 381 BG 8AF Began service April 28, 1944; lost October 10, 1944. NASM

Virgins Delight B-17 42-3352 94 BG 8AF Lost on a mission to Solingen November 30, 1943. NASM

Virgin Sturgeon B-17 42-30334 390 BG 8 AF Lost on a mission to Frankfurt January 29, 1944. NASM

Hulcher's Vultures B-17 42-39845 388BG 8AF Lost April 28, 1944. NASM

Wallaroo B-17 42-3029 303 BG 8AF Began service April 9, 1943; lost on a mission to Pas De Calais January 14, 1944. NASM

Wee Willie B-17 42-31333 322 BS 91 BG 8 AF Began service December 20, 1943; lost April 8, 1945. NASM

What's Cookin Doc? B-17 41-24525 384BG 8 AF Lost over Ludwigshafen January 7, 1944. NASM

Whirlaway B-17 381 BG NASM

Wicked Witch B-17 323 BS 91 BG 8 AF NASM

The Wild Hare B-17 42-31515 91BG 324BS 8 AF Began service January 21, 1944; lost on a mission to Bremen November 26, 1944. NASM

Wolfess B-17 42-29953 305 BG 8 AF Salvaged November 15, 1943. NASM

Woosh Woosh B-17 305 BG 8AF NASM

Yankee Doodle Dandy James Cagney christens a B-17 42-39953 of the 390 BG. Lost to Leipzig April 29, 1944. NASM

Yankee Doodle B-17 41-9023 97 BG 414BS 8AF NASM

Yankee Rebel B-17 381 BG 8AF NASM

You've Had It B-17 43-39143 452 BG 8AF NASM

You've Had It! B-17 NASM

Yankee Gal B-17 42-29557 384 BG 8AF Salvaged October 23, 1943. NASM

Yankee Gal B-17 43-37844 91 BG 8AF NASM

The Zoot Suiters B-17 42-30235 95BG 8AF NASM

Zootie Cutie B-17-G 43-37616 NASM

B-17 NASM

———***But Right*** B-17 NASM

B-17 NASM

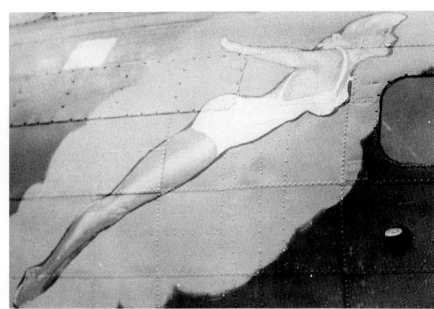

B-17 NASM

B-17 NASM

————**Pride** B-17 NASM

Anxious Angel B-17-G 91 BG 8 AF AFM

Bam Bam B-17 42-37893 Joined the 303 BG November 18, 1943. AFM

Better Duck B-17 43-8990 95 BG 8 AF Flew 53 missions prior to returning to the US in July 1945. Lt. Cook, looking from the window, was lost on May 7, 1945 (the day before V-E Day) on a chow hound mercy mission to northern Europe. It is believed that the plane was lost to small arms fire. The aircraft—B-17 44-8640—was the last 8 AF plane lost during the war. *Cook Collection*

Big Dick B-17 8 AF Named for the dice roll "Big Dick from Dixie." AFM

The Biggest Bird B-17 AFM

Bomb Boogie B-17 42-5763 401 BS 91 BG 8 AF Began March 9, 1943; lost to Stuttgart September 6, 1943. AFM

Bomber Dear B-17-C-45-BO 42-97234 91 BG 8 AF AFM

Cabin in the Sky B-17-F 42-30338 571 BS 390 BG 8 AF Major Brown looks out of the cabin February 25, 1945. AFM

Cindy B-17 2-5821 379 BG 8 AF One of the original 379th aircraft. Lost to Gelsenkirchen August 12, 1943. *AFM*

Dear Mom B-17 *AFM*

Dry Martini & the Cocktail Kids (The 4th) B-17-F 364 BS 305 BG 8 AF Note two swans plus twenty fighter kills. *AFM*

Fearless Fosdick B-17-G 43-37890 401 BG 8 AF *AFM*

Fitch's Bandwagon B-17 42-107043 401 BG 8 AF Began March 23, 1944; beyond repair after crash two weeks later. *AFM*

The Floose B-17 42-97298 358 BS 303 BG 8 AF Had over 100 missions when it was destroyed in a wheels-up landing. *AFM*

60

D Day Doll B-17 447 BG 8 AF In the Arizona desert waiting to be sold for scrap. *AFM*

Flak-Happy B-17 92 BG 327 BS 8 AF *AFM*

Man O War II B-17 42-38083 91 BG 8 AF Named after the famous race horse. It joined the 91st January 10, 1944; failed to return from a mission to Merseburg November 2, 1944. *AFM*

Sheriff's Posse B-17 42-97151 91 BG 8 AF 1st Lt. Robert E. Sheriff of Cleveland, OH, polishes the star on his aircraft's nose art. Joined the 91st March 3, 1944; declared beyond repair after a crash landing March 23, 1944. *AFM*

Goonie B-17 11BG 98 BS Named for the Goonie Bird, which had a semi-crash landing style. *AFM*

Grim Reaper B-17 97 BG North Africa. The Grim Reaper had flown 35 missions when this photo was taken. 7 crew members have purple hearts and have shot down 10 aircraft, 6 on one mission. Over Trapani, Sicily, 3 gunners were wounded, one engine lost, and a fire broke out in the bomb bay area. *AFM*

Hikin' for Home B-17 42-107027 91 BG 8 AF 73 Joined April 7, 1944, named "Anne." *AFM*

Holy Terror III B-17 100 BG 8 AF *AFM*

Impatient Virgin B-17 42-3273 95 BG 8 AF The nose art seems to express the mood of the aircraft after a nose-down landing December 24, 1943. *University of Texas at Dallas Collection.*

Impatient Virgin B-17-F 306 BG *AFM*

Iza Vailable Too B-17 42-97254 360 BS 303 BG 8 AF AFM

Goin Jessies B-17 42-31051 100 BG 8 AF Lost March 6, 1944,

Lady Helen of Wimpole B-17 91 BG 8AF Lady Helen christens her. B-17. AFM

Lakanuki B-17 42-4176 379 BG 8 AF Interned in Sweden January 5, 1944. AFM

Little Patches B-17 42-31578 401 BS 91 BG 8 AF Joined the 91st December 29, 1943; lost March 6, 1944, on a mission to Berlin. AFM

The Lucky Strike B-17 41-29923 381 BG 8 AF Began service September 11, 1943; salvaged January 5, 1944. AFM

"Naturals" B-17 42-29711 94 BG 8 AF AFM

Old Glory B-17 42-31432 303 BG 8 AF Began service January 18, 1944; lost June 22, 1944. AFM

Our Bridget B-17-G 44-6975 91 BG 8 AF AFM

Out House Mouse B-17 42-31636 Joined the 91st BG, 8th AF, March 12, 1944; returned May 25, 1945. On August 16, 1944, a German 163 B rocket fighter flew alongside for 30 seconds without attacking . . . probably checking out the nose art! AFM

The Peacemaker B-17 43-37552 91 BG 8AF Began service June 2, 1944; salvaged April 13, 1945. AFM

Perpetual Help B-17 43-38887 457 BG 8 AF First named "Perpetual Hell" November 4, 1944—Note the photo taped onto the aircraft—returned to the US during May 1945. AFM

Piccadilly Lilly II B-17 42-37800 100 BG 8 AF Named for the Piccadilly Circus in London. Beyond repair June 28, 1944. *AFM*

Queenie B-17 42-31353 91 BG 8 AF Began service December 20, 1943; lost over Berlin April 29, 1944. *AFM*

Raging Red B-17 42-31353 91 BG 8 AF Joined the 91st June 21, 1943; lost to Schweinfurt August 17, 1943. *AFM*

Rebel's Revenge B-17 42-29750 Joined the 91st BG, 8 AF, August 24, 1943; lost over Emden September 27, 1943. *AFM*

Rebel's Revenge In flight. *NASM*

The Red Gremlin B-17 *AFM*

Redwing B-17 43-38088 91 BG 8 AF *AFM*

Ruby's Raiders B-17 44-6483 385 BG 9 AF This aircraft was named for Cpl. Ruby Newell of Longbeach, CA. Voted the most beautiful WAC in England. *AFM*

Royal Flush! B-17 42-6087 100 BG 8 AF Note the face of the joker and the sixteen kills for twenty bombing missions. *AFM*

Scheherazade B-17 42-29886 379 BG 8 AF Failed to return from Frankfurt January 29, 1944. *AFM*

Shackeroo! II B-17 42-29708 94 BG 8 AF First assigned to the 95th BG, it was named after joining the 94th in May 1943. *AFM*

Shedonwanna? B-17 42-30201 388 BG 8 AF Lt. Baum looks out of the left front side gunners port sometime in 1943. Lost September 6, 1943, on a mission to Stuttgart. *NASM*

Snap! Crackle! Pop! B-17 41-24620 303 BG 8 AF Lost over St. Nazaire January 3, 1943. AFM

Snoozin' Suzan B-17 AFM

Stage Door Canteen B-17 42-31990 381 BG 535 BS 8 AF Christened by Mary Churchill April 23, 1944, along with George Parks, Vivien Leigh and Laurence Olivier. Flew over 100 missions before returning to the US in June 1945. AFM

Sit n Git B-26 AFM

Spirit of '44 B-17 42-37940 91BG 8AF Began service December 13, 1943; salvaged January 16, 1944. AFM

Stud Duck B-17 100 BG & 94 BG 8 AF AFM

Superman B-17 The oldest ship in the oldest group in North Africa, has had over seventeen engines, 300 flak holes and six purple hearts with no fatalities. *AFM*

The Sweater Girl B-17 379 BG 8 AF AFM

Tondelayo B-17 42-29896 379 BG 8 AF Failed to return from Stuttgart September 6, 1943. *AFM*

The Uncouth Bastard B-17 305 BG 8 AF *AFM*

Victory Queen B-17-G 91 BG 8 AF *AFM*

Windy City Avenger B-17 42-3037 384 BG & 305 BG 8 AF Arrived at the 384 BG September 20, 1943; declared beyond repair October 12, 1943. *AFM*

Wabash Cannonball B-17 42-29947 Served with the 100 BG, 300 BG, 91 BG, 388 BG and survived the war. *AFM*

Wahoo B-17-F 41-24468 369 BS 306 BG 8 AF 1st Lt. Robert P. Riordan of El Paso, TX, gives the war cry after landing with flak damage after a raid on Lillie, France. November 12, 1942. Later destroyed on landing, June 26, 1943. *AFM*

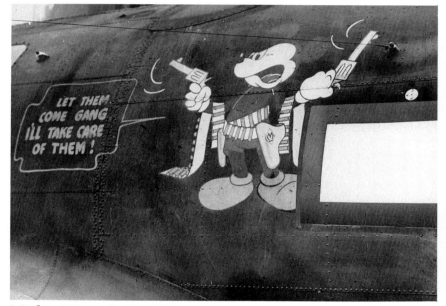

Mickey Mouse B-17 AFM

B-17 AFM

The Joker's Wild B-17 41-24521 AFM

General "Ike" B-17 42-97061 91BG 8 AF Note prop damage. AFM

Scarlett O'Hara B-17 379BG 8AF AFM

Bonnie-B B-17 42-31483 303BG 8AF Began service January 1, 1944; salvaged September 9, 1944. AFM

Dragon Lady B-17 42-30836 385 BG 8AF Lost over Pas de Calais February 13, 1944. NASM

Pistol Packin' Mama B-17 390 BG 8 AF Hoffman, May and Morris display their jackets. AFM

100 missions, 13 ships, 5 aircraft NASM

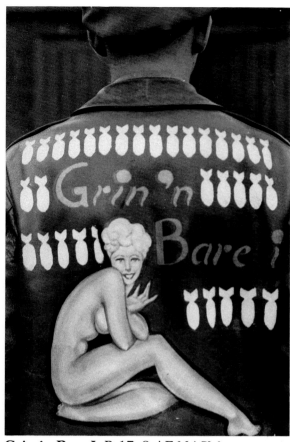

Grin 'n Bare It B-17 8 AF NASM

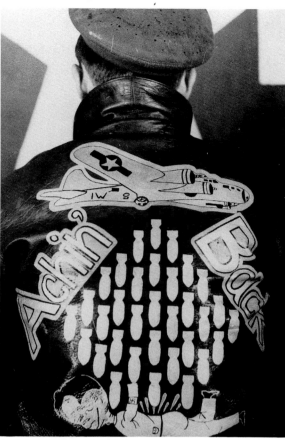

Achin' Back NASM

Belle O' The Brawl B-17 401 BG 8 AF NASM

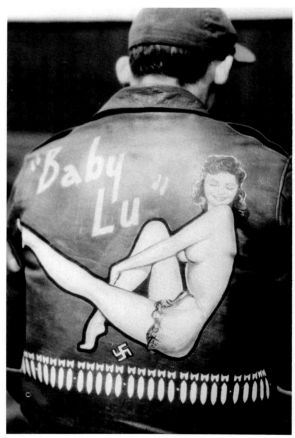

Baby Lu B-17 401 BG 8 AF NASM

Fancy Nancy B-17 401 BG 8 AF NASM

Gaposis B-17 401 BG 8 AF NASM

Miss Wing Ding B-17 401 BG 8 AF NASM

Mary Alice Gnatzi-Knight B-17 401 BG
8 AF NASM

Off We Go NASM

Prop Wash B-17 401 BNG 8 AF NASM

Patent Pending B-17 401 BG 8 AF NASM

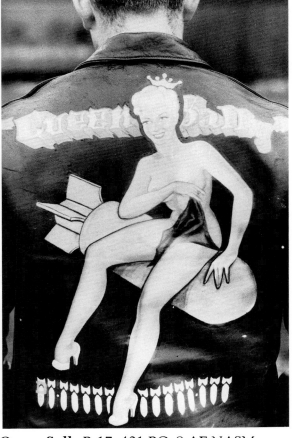

Queen Sally B-17 401 BG 8 AF NASM

BTO of ETO (Big Time Operator of the European Theater of Operations) B-17 401 BG 8 AF *NASM*

Rosie's Sweat Box B-17 401 BG 8 AF *NASM*

Sweet Dreams B-17 401 BG 8 AF *NASM*

Swingin' on a Star B-17 401 BG 8 AF *NASM*

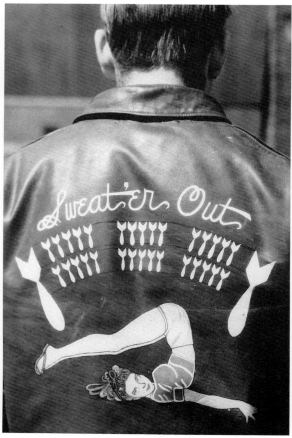

Sweat'er Out B-17 401 BG 8 AF *NASM*

Shade Ruff B-17 401 BG 8 AF *NASM*

Snicklefritz NASM

Screamin' Demon B-17 401 BG 8A F NASM

Tag A Long B-17 8 AF NASM

Twannggg B-17 NASM

Time'll Tell! NASM

Twang-g-g B-17 NASM

The Careful Virgin NASM

Visibility Perfect B-17 401 BG 8 AF NASM

What's Cookin B-17 401 BG 8 AF NASM

Yankee Eagle NASM

Madame Queen B-17 401 BG 8 AF AFM

The Farmer's Daughter B-17 AFM

Hell's Angel Out of Chute 13 B-17 401
BG 8AF NASM

Slick Chick B-17 401 BG 8AF AFM

Heavenly Body-Little Friend P-51 AFM

Fitch's Bandwagon B-17 401 BG 8 AF
AFM

Just Once More B-17-G 44-8854 94 BG 333 BS 8 AF CAF/G. Valant

Major Byron Trent in front of *Just Once More* at Rougham, England, 1945. *B. Trent*

CAF collection

Target for Tonight B-17 CAF/G. *Valant*

Double Trouble B-24 44-42460 436 BS 7 BG 10 AF The crew formed in March 1944 at Hammer Field, Fresno, CA, and took B-24 training at Muros AFB. They were assigned to the CBI theater in India. This is the plane that bombed the bridge over the River Kwai. CAF/G. *Valant*

Sleepy Time Gal B-24-M-15 44-51030 CAF/G. Valant

Home Stretch B-24 7 BG 10 AF CAF/G. Valant

Mission Completed B-17 CAF/G. Valant

Yellow Fever B-24-M 44-50803 374 BS 308 BG 14 AF CAF/G. Valant

Forever Amber B-24-J 42-73188 374 BS 308 BG 14 AF CAF/G. Valant

You Speak B-24 454 BG 737 BS 15 AF
Italy. CAF/G. Valant

Lassie I'm Home B-17 7 BG 436 BS 10 AF CAF/G. Valant

Miss Yourlovin B-24 CAF/G. Valant

Lady Luck B-24 CAF/G. Valant

Mutz CAF/G. Valant

Nobby's Harriet J B-17 CAF/G. Valant

B-17 CAF/G. Valant

Mis Behavin B-17 CAF/G. Valant

CAF/G. Valant

Yankee Girl B-16 42-7522 506 BS 44 BG CAF/G. Valant

B-17-G 44-6779 CAF/G. Valant

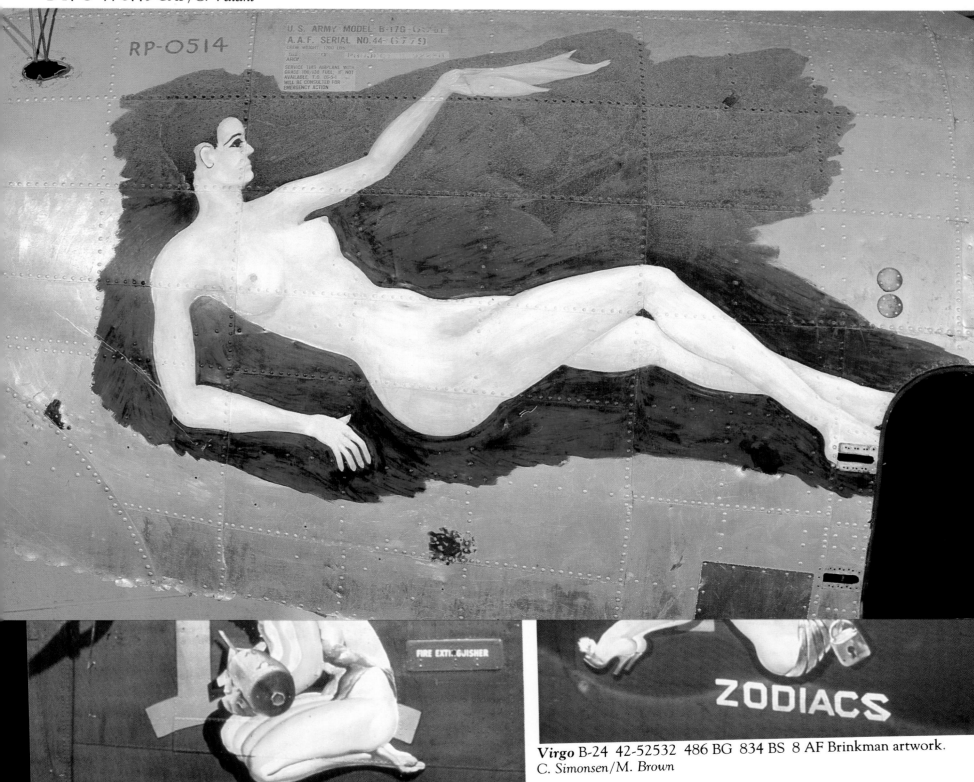

Virgo B-24 42-52532 486 BG 834 BS 8 AF Brinkman artwork.
C. Simonsen/M. Brown

Leo B-24 486 BG 834 BS 8 AF Brinkman artwork. C.S./M artwork. *C. Simonsen/M. Brown*

Libra B-24 42-52508 486 BG 834 BS 8 AF Brinkman nose art. *C. Simonsen/M. Brown*

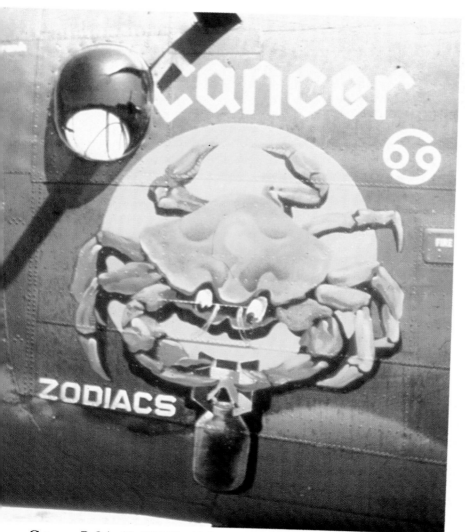

Cancer B-24 42-52665 486 BG 834 BS 8 AF Brinkman artwork. *C. Simonsen/M. Brown*

90

Varga Girls

Night Mission B-24-D 42-40891 Was assigned to the 397 bombardment squadron and patrolled from Managua to Salinas, Ecuador, and all over the Caribbean. *Esquire.* CAF/G. *Valant*

"O-O-Nothing!" B-24 *Esquire.* CAF/M. *Querin*

Sack Time B-24-M 44-50797 308 BG *Esquire.* CAF/G. *Valant*

Ole Baldy B-24 8 AS *C. Simonsen*

Bobby Sox B-17-G 44-8158 94 BG 332 BS 8 AF *C. Simonsen*

Miss Manchester B-26-C 320 BG 441 BS The crest was "unofficial" and used in World War II only. *C. Simonsen*

Belle Ringer B-26-C 320 BG 441 BS *C. Simonsen*

Tondelayo B-24 487 BG 8 AF Artist: Sgt. Daune Bryers *C. Simonsen*

Old Rusty P-38 1st FTR GP Pilot W. G. Campbell. *C. Simonsen*

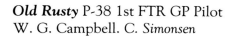

Bonnie P-47 56 FTR GP 61 FTR SQN 8 AF *C. Simonsen*

Lay or Bust B-17-G 42-97230 100 BG
C. Simonsen

Our Gal Sal B-17-G 42-31767 100 BG Scrapped at Kingman,
AZ, 1947. *C. Simonsen*

Miss Barbara B-17-F 41-24519 AFM

P-47 318 FTR GP 333 FTR SQN *C. Simonsen*

Shady Lady B-24 44-40439 8 AF
C. Simonsen

Peace Maker B-29 19 BG C. Simonsen

Big Shmoo B-29 19 BG From the comic strip "Li'l Abner" by Al Capp. *C. Simonsen*

Southern Comfort B-29 19 BG C. Simonsen

Mairzy Doates B-24 8 AF Armour plate added to help protect the pilot covers a portion of the original artwork. *C. Simonsen*

Bockscar B-29 Second plane to drop an atomic bomb on Japan, it is in the Air Force Museum, Dayton, Ohio. *AFM/G. Valant*

Senta A Pua NASM

Finito Benito Next Hirohito B-25 Photo taken over Italy. *NASM*

96

A Bit o' *Lace* B-17-G-40-VE 42-97976 709 BS 447 BG Painted by Nicholas Fingelly from a sketch by Milton Caniff. Miss Lace was a character in Caniff's "Male Call," which ran in the army camp newspapers. Miss Lace became a favorite character with the GIs because she preferred enlisted men to officers, but called them "General," or "Admiral." Another Caniff character that was widely copied was "the Dragon Lady." C. Simonsen

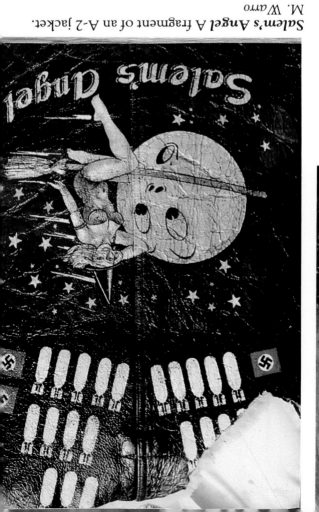

Salem's Angel A fragment of an A-2 jacket.
M. Warro

The Shack B-24-J-CO-156 44-40398 753 BS 487 BG Painted by Burne Bryers. C. Simonsen

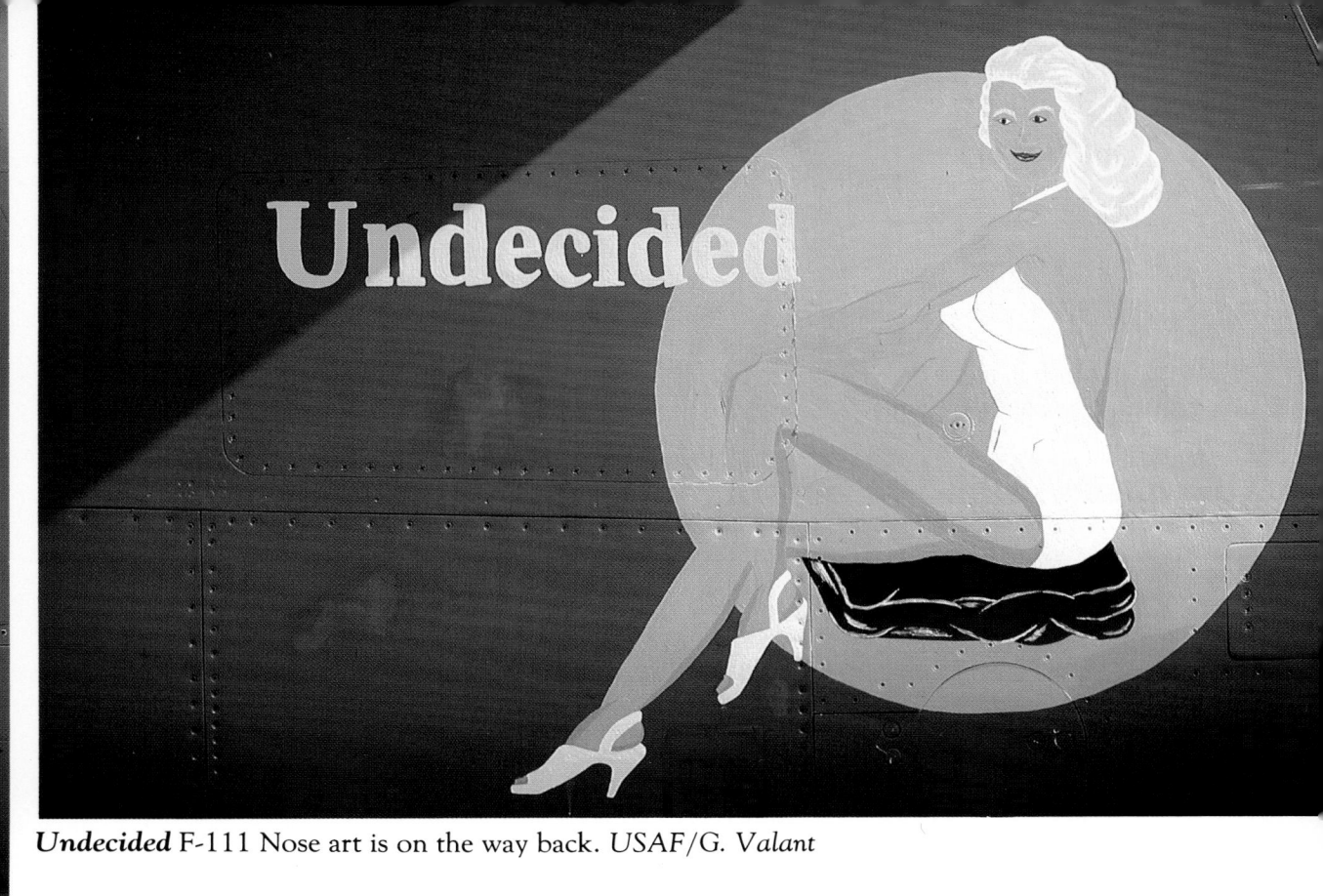

Undecided F-111 Nose art is on the way back. *USAF/G. Valant*

Lucky Strike F-111 This artwork also flew on a B-24 in the Philippines in 1944. *USAF/G. Valant*

Dragon Lady B-24 *C. Simonsen*

Cocktail Hour B-24-J-161-CO 44-40428 43BG 403 BS *C. Simonsen*

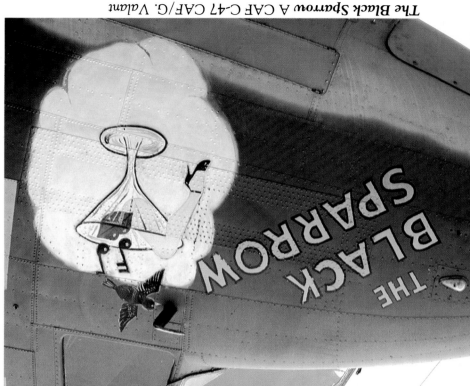

The Black Sparrow A CAF C-47 CAF/G. Valant

Daisy Mae Contemporary nose art on a B-25. CAF/G. Valant

Big Ole Brew N Little Ole You B-25
CAF/G. Valant

Sentimental Journey B-17 CAF/G. Valant

During WW II, it was common practice for AAF combat flyers to paint their A-2 leather flying jackets in various schemes, ranging from amateur to professional quality. This A-2, painted by the donor, is the most beautiful example in the Air Force Museum collection. On the back are bombs depicting his 35 missions and a painting of his "girl back home."

A-2 bomber jacket on display at the Air Force Museum. *AFM*

This artwork was done in Oklahoma City prior to departure for the South Pacific. *AFM*

Beat Up Bastard (Bub for short) B-29 19 BG *R. Mann*

Never Hoppen B-29 19 BG *R. Mann*

105

Boulder Buff B-24 AFM

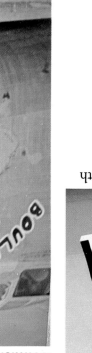

Strawberry Bitch B-24 Painted in US prior to going to North Africa. Now in the Air Force Museum. AFM/H. V. Morgan

World War II production poster as it hangs in the Air Force Museum at Dayton, Ohio. Note the nose art. AFM/G. Valant

Dream Girl Restored A-26 "Invader" at the Air Force Museum. AFM/G. Valant

B-17 over England NASM

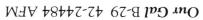

Our Gal B-29 42-24484 AFM

War Goddess B-24 93BG 8AF AFM

B-17s with fighter escort somewhere over Europe. NASM

B-24s form up on a lead ship. Note the colorful markings on the lead ship. After the formation was set, the lead ship (usually a tired veteran) would return to base. NASM

Lou IV and other P-51s fly deep escort for B-17s over Germany. Note the extra fuel tanks under the wings. These could be released for air combat. NASM

Fifinella B-17 8 AF The name Fifinella means female gremlin. The first Fifinella was reported at Kelly Field, TX, around 1923. The RAF saw the first one in England in 1928, and since then every Air Force in the world has had them. Flyers claim that gremlins live near airports and like to collect nuts and bolts from aircraft. There are a few good gremlins, but we fear that most are bad, as they tend to steal important nuts and bolts. The Fifinella are exceptionally beautiful and live off the pimento stuffing found in martini olives, which give them the delicate complexions. NASM

Ferocious Frankie P-51 Lt. Col. Wallace Hopkins flies over England. NASM

Tom Paine B-17-F 42-30790 388 BG 8 AF NASM

Schnozzle B-17-G-1Q-VE 42-45611 381 BG 8 AF. Began with 381st January 22, 1944; salvaged November 27, 1944. NASM

Pappy Recon plane with Li'l Abner's Pappy sitting under a B-17 in England. NASM

5 Grand B-17 43-37716 96 BG 8AF. The 5,000th B-17 produced by Boeing after Pearl Harbor. It was signed by the factory workers and flew in combat as shown. It survived the war, but not the smelters; it was scrapped at Kingman, AZ, in 1947. The plane had "5 Grand" painted on both sides of the nose, but the crew called her "Easter Egg." NASM

Little Miss Mischief B-17 42-97880 91 BG 8 AF Nose art painted by Tony Starcer, who did over 130 aircraft. Crash landing April 1945, Bassingbourn, England. NASM

Lonesome Polecat Jr B-24 China. NASM

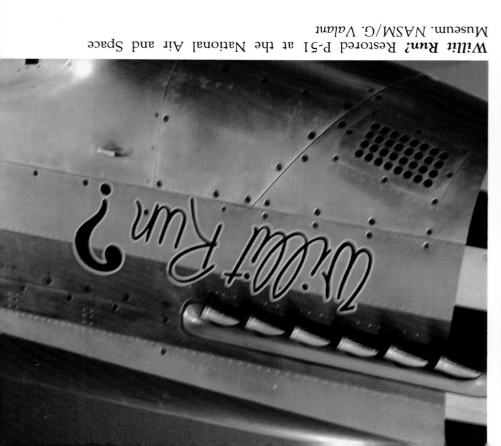

Willit Run? Restored P-51 at the National Air and Space Museum. NASM/G. Valant

Idiots' Delight B-17 42-30301 94 BG 8 AF NASM

Alabama Express B-26 NASM

OH-7 B-25 Photo taken in North Africa. NASM

Wash's Tub B-24 NASM

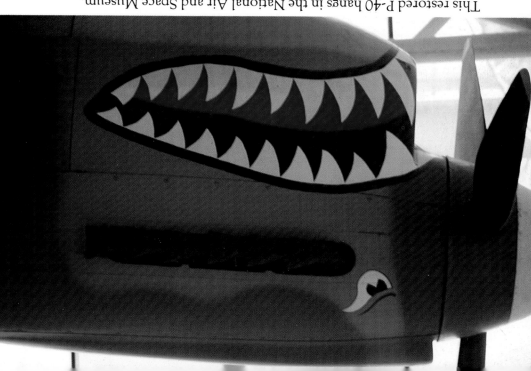

This restored P-40 hangs in the National Air and Space Museum, Washington, D.C. NASM/G. Valant

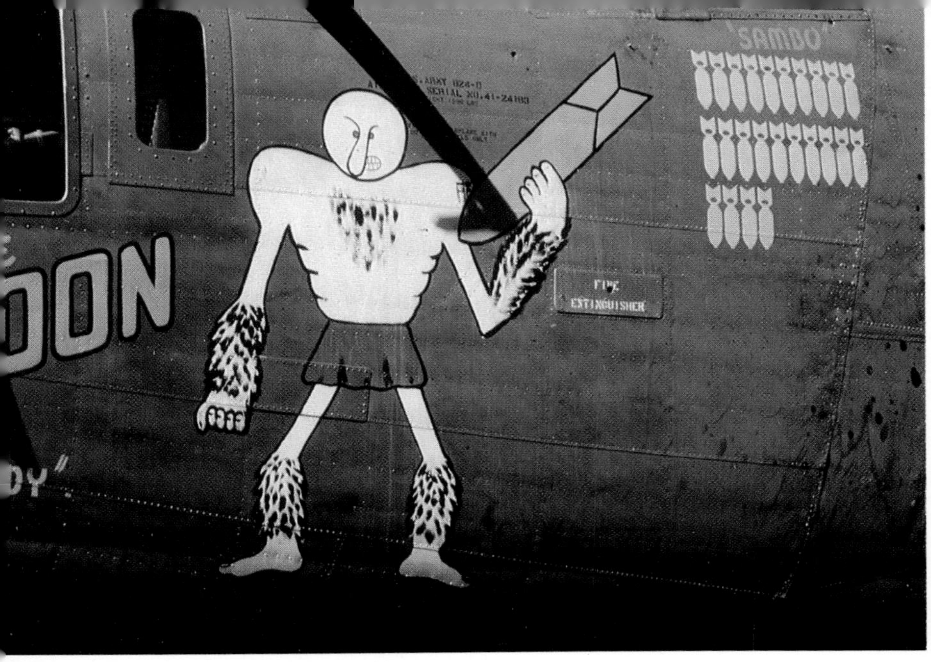

The "Goon" B-24 NASM

Hookem Cow B-24-H 42-95128 458 BG 755 BS 8 AF Artwork
by Harold Johnston. Crashed April 14, 1945. NASM

NASM

Little Cheezer B-17 401 BG 8 AF AFM

Diabolical Angel B-17 401 BG 612 BS 8 AF AFM

Veni-Vidi-Vici B-17 401 BG 8 AF AFM

Tantalizing Takeoff B-17 AFM

A-Vailable B-24 NASM

Boot in the Ass B-24 AFM

Tropic Knight B-24 Note crew lists. NASM

The Angry Angel B-24 7 BG 9 BS 10 AF *Leo Huken*

Axis Nightmare B-24-D 41-24138 AFM

Snow White and the Seven Dwarfs B-24 343 BS 98 BG 9 AF
NASM

Prince Charming B-24-D 343 BS 98 BG 9 AF NASM

Grumpy B-24-D 42-41825 343 BS 98 BG 9AF AFM

Happy B-24-D 42-40256 343 BS 98 BG 9 AF AFM

Sneezy B-24-D 41-3795 343 BS 98 BG 9 AF *AFM*

Sleepy B-24-D 41-11701 343 BS 98 BG 9 AF AFM

Bashful B-24-D 41 11770 343 BS 98 BG 99 AF AFM

Dopey B-24-D 42-40268 343 BS 98 BG 9 AF AFM

Doc B-24-D 41-11921 343 BS 98 BG 9 AF NASM

The Witch B-24-D 1-11834 343 BS 98 BG 9 AF Note mission symbols. *AFM*

Big Time Operator B-24-J 44-40737 AFM

The Blind Bat B-24-D 42-11738 AFM

Bodacious Critter B-24 AFM

The Bad Penny B-24 AFM

Boomerang B-24 7 BG 9 BS 10 AF L. Huken

Balls o' Fire B-25 AFM

Buzzzz Job B-24 AFM

Bourbon Boxcar B-24 AFM

Barbara Jean B-24 AFM

Final Objective B-24 AFM

Feathermerchant's Folly B-24 AFM

Flying Fannie B-24 AFM

Glamouras' B-24 Pronounced "Glamour Ass" AFM

The Gremlin B-24-D 41-24111 AFM

Gang Bang B-24 C. P. Dicecco

"Hot" To Go B-24 7 BG 9 BS 10 AF L. Huken

Hilo Hattie B-24 AFM

It Aint So Funny B-24 NASM

Innocent Infant B-24-L 44-49649 308 BG AFM

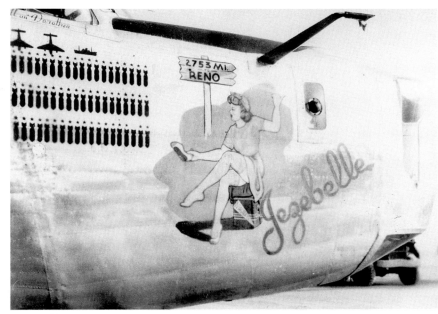

Jezebelle B-24 AFM

Jungle Queen AL 640 6 BG AFM

Kongo Kutie C-87 (Cargo B-24) 9th AF AFM

Kansas City Kitty B-24-L 44-41480

King's X B-24 AFM

"Little Flower" B-24 AFM

Lonesome Lady B-24 AFM

Luscious Lace B-24 7 BG 9 BS 10 AF L. Huken

Lili Marlene B-24 AFM

Munda Belle B-24 AFM

Miss Carriage B-24-D AFM

Marlene B-24 AFM

Miss Dorothy B-24 AFM

Miss Lace B-24 AFM

Miss Tennessee B-24 7 BG 9 BS 10 AF L. Huken

Miss Liberty B-24 AFM

Miss Beryl B-24 308 BG AFM

Miss Hilda B-24 7 BG 9 BS 10 AF L. Huken

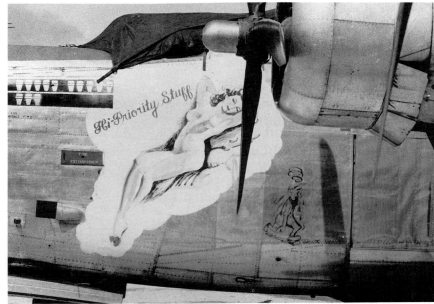

Hi Priority Stuff B-24-J 44-40967 Photo recon. Note cameras
for mission markers. AFM

Not in Stock B-24 AFM

Nana B-24 566 BS 389 BG *T. Bivens*

Photo Fanny B-24 Photo recon. AFM

Pistol Packing Mama B-24 *W. Hughs*

Princess Konocti B-24 566 BS 389 BG Note "Bombi" the fawn. *T. Bivens*

Princess Konocti B-24 566 BS 389 BG The other side of the plane. *T. Bivens*

Pacific Tramp III B-24 AFM

Pappy's Passion B-24 AFM

Pacific Passion B-24 AFM

Patched Up Piece B-24 Photo recon. AFM

The Peter Heater B-24 AFM

Queen Mae B-24

Red Butt B-24 W. Hughs

The Rip Snorter B-24 20th combat mapping squad. *AFM*

Ready Willing and Able B-24-D 41-41078 Shot down over Nadzab, crew bailed out safely. *Albert Marston*

Sweetest of Texas B-24 *AFM*

Sluggin' Sal B-24 *AFM*

Sitting Pretty B-24 *AFM*

Slammin' Spammy B-24 Named in honor of the GI's favorite food—Spam. *AFM*

Settin Pretty B-24-L 44-41429 308 BG Note the camels that denote each trip "over the hump" (over the Himalayas). AFM

Satan's Baby B-24 AFM

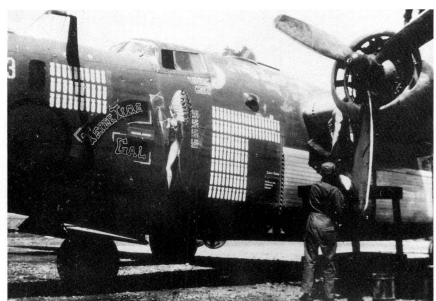

Short Run! B-24 AFM

Tepee Time Gal B-24 AFM

Tennessee Belle B-24 AFM

Wild Honey B-24 W. Hughs

Wham! Bam! "Thank You Ma'm" B-24 AFM

Wolf Pack B-24 AFM

The Wango Wango Bird B-24 Note exhaust note. AFM

The Wolf B-24 AFM

B-24-J 44-40796 This is a squadron marker. Note the instruction at the air access port "Remember Me." AFM

B-24 Nose art in progress. W. Hughs

B-24 Vargas-inspired nose art. *AFM*

B-24 **Before** *C. P. Dicecco*

B-24 **After** (other side of plane). *C. P. Dicecco*

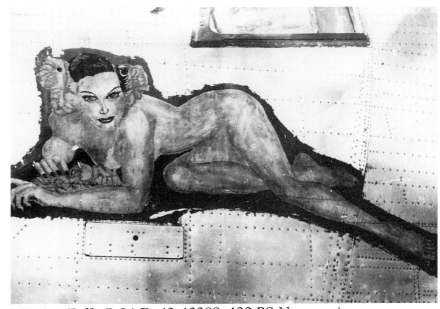

Mission Belle B-24-D 42-40389 400 BS Nose art in progress. *AFM*

A-Tisket A-Tasket A G-I Casket B-24 Somewhere in the South Pacific; armorers prepare frag bombs for loading. *NASM*

As-cend Charlie B-24 *NASM*

130

Alfred II B-24 NASM

Angel Face 3rd B-24 NASM

Arkansas Traveler B-24 NASM

"Bat Out of Hell" B-24-J 44-40526 11BG Guam May 4, 1945. NASM

Bugs Bomby Jr. B-24-L-5-CO 44-41466 11 BG Guam. NASM

Bundles for Japan B-24 Note witch's broom is a 50-cal. machine gun. NASM

Bomb Baby B-24-J 42-72976 Photo taken on Kwajalein July 1944. NASM

Baby Bug B-24 490 BG 8 AF NASM

Barrel House Bessie B-24 July 1944. NASM

Battling Hornet B-24 Kwajalein July 1944. NASM

Bird's Eye View B-24 11 BG Guam May 1945. NASM

Biscay Belle B-24 479 Anti-submarine GP 8 AF NASM

Blond Bomber B-24 41-11095 NASM

Bodacious Idjit and H.T. B-24 11 BG Guam May 1945. Caption "Writ By Hand X an' Seal't Wit' Terbaccu Joos." NASM

Bomb Babe B-24 NASM

Bombs Lullaby B-24 42-72988 Play on "Brahm's Lullaby." NASM

Bomberang B-24-D 41-29722 8 AF Pronounced "Bomber-Rang." NASM

"Briney Marlin" B-24 458 BG 8 AF Lt. Lester C. Marlin with his B-24. NASM

Bugs Buggy B-24 *NASM*

The Bull B-24 *NASM*

The Butcher Boy B-24-D 41-24108 *NASM*

Heaven Can Wait B-24 *NASM*

Calamity Jane B-25 Somewhere in India. *NASM*

Celhalopdos B-24 A slight misspelling of "Cephalopoda" of which the octopus is a member. *NASM*

Contrary Mary! B-24 NASM

Crash Kids B-24 NASM

Come Closer B-24 Photo taken in Saipan. NASM

Cowbird B-24 NASM

Censored nose art on a B-24 NASM

Darlin Dutchess & the 10 Dukes B-24 42-64500 NASM

Hit-Parade B-24 NASM

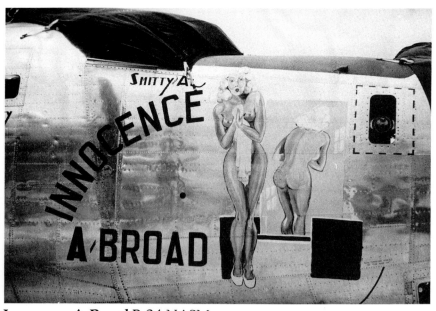

Innocence A-Broad B-24 NASM

Kansas Cyclone B-24 26 BS 11 BG NASM

Kay Rashun B-24-J 42-70236 Photo taken on Kwajalein July 1944. Named after the GI's 2nd favorite meal (after Spam). NASM

"Kickapoo-Kid" B-24-J 42-72003 Kwajalein July 1944. NASM

Lucky Dog B-24 11 BG Guam May 1945. NASM

Lady Leone B-24 NASM

Late Date B-24 NASM

"Lakanooki" B-24-D 41-24810 Pronounced "Lack A Nooki." *NASM*

Lil Audrey B-24-J 42-79416 Aircraft completed 100 missions in the Marianas. *NASM*

The Little General B-24 NASM

Little Hiawatha B-24 Funafuti, Ellice Island. Gen. Hale and B-24 crew with a bomb autographed by Bing Crosby. *NASM*

Little Red B-24 NASM

Lizzy Belle B-24 490 BG 8 AF NASM

Mad Russian B-24 NASM

Madame Pele B-24 42-109951 26 BS 11 BG 7 AF Purchased with funds raised by Hawaiian school children and named for the Hawaiian goddess of fire. NASM

Merry Boozer B-24-J 42-109945 Kwajalein July 1944. NASM

Michigan B-24-J-161-CO 44-40429 43 BG NASM

Miss Bee Haven B-24-J-CO-2 42-72982 *NASM*

The Missouri Mule B-24 494 BG Col. Kelly of the 494th stands besides the wrecked B-24 April 10, 1945, Angaur Island *NASM*

Murphy's Mother In Law B-24 Worse than Murphy's Law (if anything can go wrong—it will). *NASM*

My Bunnie II B-24 8 AF *NASM*

My Diversion B-24 *NASM*

Near Miss B-24 *NASM*

Nipponese Clipper B-24 38 BS 30 BG NASM

Oklahoma Gal B-24-J 42-50567 8 AF Slight undercarriage damage after crash landing at Bungay, Norfolk, England, August 27, 1944. NASM

Out of This World B-24-J 44-40601 11 BG NASM

Photo Queen B-24 Photo recon. NASM

Pistol Pakin Mamma B-24 Kwajalein 1944. NASM

Play Boy B-24 NASM

142

Pleasure Bent B-24 AFM

Plunderbus B-24 NASM

Rose of Juarez B-24 8 AF NASM

Riot Call B-24 NASM

Ruff Knights B-24 11 BG Guam May 1945. NASM

Ruthless Ruthie B-24 8 AF Note armor plate add-on over nose art. NASM

Sack Time Sal II B-24 NASM

Salty Sal B-24 Kwajalein July 1944. NASM

Secrut Weapin B-24 42-100224 NASM

Shady Lady B-24-J 8 AF Wrecked November 27, 1944. NASM

Smokey Stover B-24 NASM

Snootie Cutie B-24 490 BG 8 AF Lt. Holden and crew. NASM

The Squaw B-24 8 AF Crewman inspects flak damage. *NASM*

"Tail Winds" B-24 8 AF *NASM*

Tarfu B-24 42-109933 Kwajalein. Pronounced "Things are Really Fouled Up." *NASM*

Temptation B-24-I 44-40617 *NASM*

Thar She Blows III B-24 *NASM*

Thar She Blows B-24-D 42 BS 11 BG July 1943 Kualoa, Oahu. *Albert Marston*

145

Tropical Trollop B-24 NASM

12 Targets to Tokyo B-24 NASM

Umbriago! B-24 NASM

Virgin Vampire B-24 Note prop damage. NASM

The Vulgar Virgin B-24 41-24192 NASM

USAFI B-24 8 AF NASM

Wabbit Twansit B-24 Kwajalein July 1944. *NASM*

Wild Ass Ride B-24 11 BG Guam May 1945. *NASM*

Wolf B-25 *NASM*

"Wolf-Pack" B-25 43 BG February 1944 Papua-New Guinea. *NASM*

Worth Fighting For B-24 *NASM*

You Bet! B-24 *NASM*

The Jeeter Bug B-24-J 44-40661 Marianas Island. *NASM*

B-24 *NASM*

B-24 *NASM*

B-24 *NASM*

B-24 42-109838 *NASM*

B-24 *NASM*

B-24 Nose art in progress, note photo taped to plane. *NASM*

B-24 Crew stands for 100th mission photo. *NASM*

B-24 *NASM*

The Superchief B-24 Palawan Island. *NASM*

"This Above All" B-24 *NASM*

Sexy Sue II B-24-D 41-23925 98 BS 11 BG Piloted by Lt. Lewis Cartwright, crash landed on Makin Island, after a mission in the Marshalls, December 18, 1943. *A. Marston*

Dogpatch Express B-24-D 41-24214 Crew and plane lost December 20, 1943, over Maloelap Atoll. *A. Marston*

The Chambermaid B-24 *NASM*

The Pelican B-24 *NASM*

Little Queen Mary B-24 NASM

Big Chief Cockeye B-24 Note: hold the photo close up and far away. AFM

Black Magic B-24 7 BG 9 BS 10 AF L. Huken

Hotcha Baby B-24 C. P. Dicecco

Hello-ver Burma B-24 7 BG 9 BS 10 AF L. Huken

Mask-A-Raid B-24 W. Hughs

151

Nocturnal Mission B-24 AFM

Over Exposed B-24 Photo recon. AFM

Peace Offering B-24 43 BG 403 BS AFM

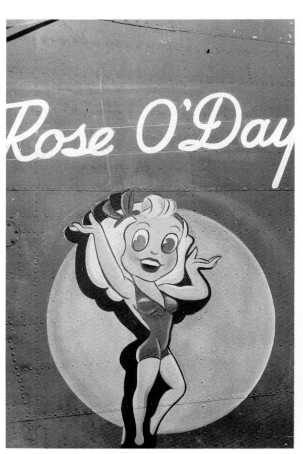

Rose O' Day B-24 AFM

Rangy Lil B-24

Shy Ann B-24 7 BG 9 BS 10 AF L. Huken

Wonderous Wanda B-24 44-40562 AFM

B-24 C. P. Dicecco

B-24 Vargas-inspired nose art. C. P. Dicecco

Brunnhilda B-24 Mechanics repair flak damage on Funafuti, Ellice Island November 17, 1943. *NASM*

B-24 Original name not known, but it offended someone. Note flak damage. *NASM*

Dangerous Critter B-24 1 BG Guam May 1945. *NASM*

Feather Merchants B-24 NASM

Going My Way B-24-J 11 BG Guam May 1944. NASM

Miss Traveler B-24 11 BG Guam May 1945. Note trunk stickers: Tokyo-Guam-Kwajalein-Tinian-Siapan. NASM

"Off We Go" B-24 Palawan Island. NASM

Pachyderm B-24 44-0141 8 AF July 17, 1944. NASM

Stormy Weather B-24 44-40556 11 BG Guam May 1945. NASM

Problem Child B-25 82BS 12BG *John Lawler*

Our Gal Ardelle B-25 82 BS 12 BG *J. Lawler*

Leroy's Joy B-25 82 BS 12 BG CBI Theater. *NASM*

Incendiary Blonde B-25 82 BS 12 BG *J. Lawler*

Bam's Mam B-25 82 BS 12 BG *J. Lawler*

Prop Wash B-25 82 BS 12 BG *J. Lawler*

155

Calcutta Commando B-25 82 BS 12 BG Note: per diem (per day) is an extra allowance given to those on temporary duty away from their normal duty station. *J. Lawler*

Miss-Behav' in B-25 82 BS 12 BG *J. Lawler*

Blonde Betty B-25 82 BS 12 BG *J. Lawler*

Vikin's Vicious Virgin B-25 82 BNS 12 BG *J. Lawler*

The Black Widow B-25 82 BS 12 BG *J. Lawler*

Go'in My Way? B-25 82 BS 12 BG *J. Lawler*

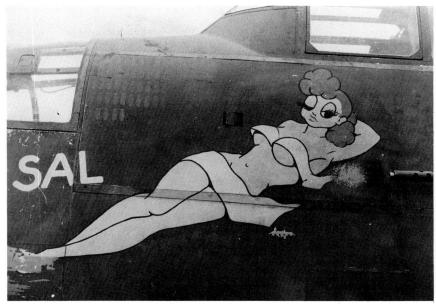

Sal B-25 82 BS 12 BG Note the paint removed by the muzzle blast of the 50-cal. machine gun. *J. Lawler*

The First Mistake B-25 AFM

Desert Warrior B-25 9 AF Note map with missions. *NASM*

Bones B-25 81 BS 12 AF Covered with names of employees of the North American aviation production plant. *NASM*

Frisky Frisco B-25 *NASM*

"Gorgeous Georgetta" B-25 81 BS 12 BG India. *NASM*

Hardships 2nd B-25 NASM

"Potch-A-Goloop" B-25 41-12562 AFM

Pluto B-25 Photo taken somewhere in Africa. NASM

The "Sad Sack" B-25 AFM

Skunk Hunter B-25 AFM

Sweat and Pray B-25 Tsgt. Alex Reams, crew chief, looks out of his aircraft. NASM

Sweater Girl B-25 18 combat mapping squad. 1943 Espiritu Santo, New Hebrides. *NASM*

Stud B-25 *NASM*

Sweet Lorraine B-25 81 BS 12 BG *NASM*

Texas Gal B-25 Note late model B-25 with cannon port. *NASM*

Valiant Virgin! B-25 *AFM*

We're Wolf B-25 71 SQ *NASM*

Golden Gate or Bust B-25 NASM

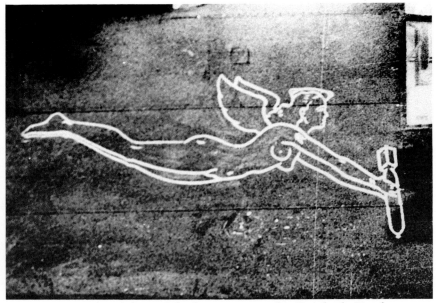

Nose art on one of the B-25s that went on the Doolittle Raid on Tokyo. *NASM*

Pride of the Yankees B-25 820 BS 41 BG NASM

Bitemontheas' B-25 AFM

B-25 NASM

Ou-La-La A-20 NASM

Jivin' Julie B-25 82 BS 12 BG *J. Lawler*

Ave Maria B-25 12 AF Aircraft flew 103 missions. *NASM*

Poopsie B-25 There are 66 little Poopsies on the aircraft, and 4 of the crew have 50 missions. *NASM*

The Marlin B-26 NASM

The Chief B-26 NASM

"Charlotte, The Harlot" B-26 41-17818 AFM

Flak Bait B-26-B 41-31773 449 BS 322 BG Flew 202 missions; now in National Air and Space Museum, NASM

"I'll Be Around" B-26 NASM

The Wolf Pack B-26 AFM

162

John Bull B-26 8 AF Lt. "John Bull" Stirling looks out of the pilot's window of his B-26. *NASM*

John Bull B-26 8 AF *NASM*

The Mad Russian B-26 381 BG 555 BS 8 AF *NASM*

Murder Inc B-26 41-18272 322 BG 8 AF Shot down, and crew captured wearing their A-2 jackets with "Murder Inc" on the back. The Germans made a propaganda film of the "Murderers" that was widely shown in Europe. After this incident, there was a review of all nose art names. *NASM*

Old Crow *NASM*

Our Baby B-26 353 BS 386 BG 8 AF *NASM*

163

Rationed Passion B-26 391 BG 8 AF NASM

Satan's Sister B-26 41-17753 AFM

The Swoose B-26 NASM

Texas Peace Maker B-26 NASM

Tootsie B-26 NASM

What's Cookin' Doc? B-26 8 AF NASM

B-26 41-34894 NASM

Zombie II B-26 NASM

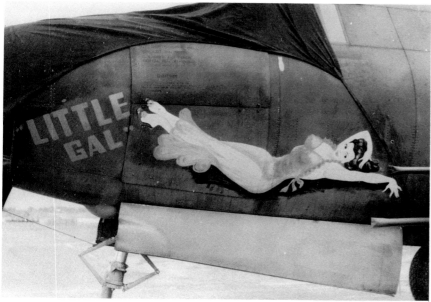

"Little Gal" B-26 AFM

"Lady Godiva" B-26-C 42-107811 AFM

Purrin' Panther B-26 AFM

Maytag Marauder B-26 AFM

Rum Buggy B-26 NASM

Pink's Lady II B-26 391 BG 8 AF NASM

Cotton A-26-C 386 BG 9 AF T. Bivens

Kiwi Boid A-26-B 43-22410 386 BG 9 AF T. Bivens

Skonk Works A-20 AFM

When The Lights Come On Again AFM

Mama Lou A-20 410 BG NASM

"Hey Stuff" P-38 367 FTR GP 8AF NASM

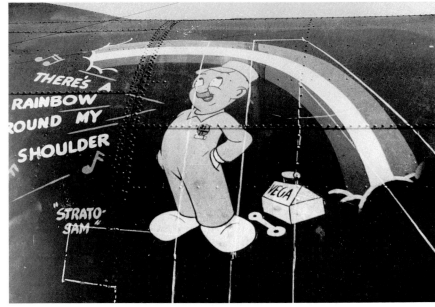

There's a Rainbow Round My Shoulder AFM

Double Busted Toby From Muskogee A-20 NASM

169

December 1944. AFM

Mary Lou AFM

Minnehaha P-51 44-11152 Lt. Shilt of the 353rd FTR GP.
NASM

Miss Fire P-47 NASM

Miss Mass P-38 367 FTR GP Note umbrellas for top cover
missions. *NASM*

Posse P-38-J Note the train kills, hats, umbrellas and brooms.
NASM

"Philbert" 3 P-38 367 FTR GP NASM

Sky Cowboy P-38-J 42-68176 AFM

Little Chief AFM

P-40 Warhawks *NASM*

P-40 Warhawks *AFM*

L-5 Recon aircraft. Some of the best artwork was on the smallest airplanes. *AFM*

Sweet Revenge 8 AF *AFM*

San Antonio Rose NASM

Dottie Anne NASM

The Goose C-47 NASM

The Swoose—It flys NASM

"The Gremlin" NASM

Dream Girl C-47 NASM

Times-A-Wastin A-20 NASM

Hell's Belle P-47 AFM

Scrapiron IV P-38 367 FTR GP NASM

Lady in the Dark P-61 Black widow night fighter *AFM*

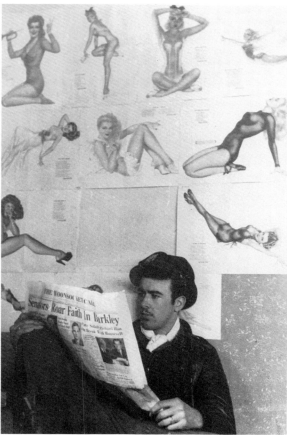

Reading the "Woonsocket Call" under an *Esquire*/Vargas calendar is Johnny Godfrey, 36 kill ace of the 4th Fighter Group. *Esquire. AFM*

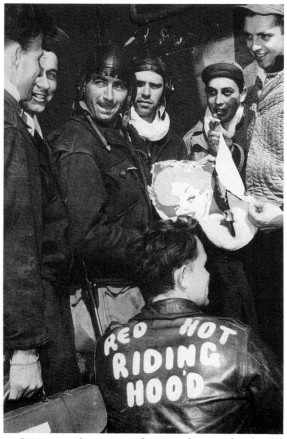

Red Hot Riding Hood Crew brings back all that is left of their bomber after a crash landing. *NASM*

The Eager Beaver III B-29 AFM

Night Mare B-29 44-87661 28 BS 19 BG Also called "Ugly" and "The Koza Kid." The B-29 was named "Ugly" when it moved to a new base near the village of Koza. When the crew laid eyes on the local cuties, they renamed the plane "The Koza Kid." This upset the local powers, and the plane was renamed again. AFM

Rock Happy B-29 AFM

Mission Inn B-29 22BG and 19 BG R. Mann

Loaded Leven B-29 Note crew names on the dice. AFM

Thunderhead B-29 AFM

Chief Mac's 10 Little Indians B-29 44-62186 AFM

Yokohama Yo-Yo B-29 42-24621 73BW AFM

Jokers Wild B-29 42-24626 AFM

Nose art in progress AFM

Capt Sam and Ten Scents B-29 19 BG AFM

Phippen's Pippins B-29 AFM

Waddy's Wagon B-29 42-24598 ASQ-5 12 AF Aircraft and crew lost returning from a raid on Tokyo January 9, 1945. *NASM*

Ramp Queen B-29 42-63513 *AFM*

Tanaka Termite B-29 *AFM*

Passion Wagon B-29 42-63324 *AFM*

Strange Cargo B-29 44-27300 Note the "Fat Man" mission markers (early nuclear bomb tests). *AFM*

Heavenly Body B-29 *AFM*

Myasis Dragon B-29 98 BG 12 AF R. Mann

Our Gal B-29 AFM

Shanghai Lil Rides Again B-29 676 BS AFM

Ogoshi Ni B-29 AFM

20th Century Sweetheart B-29 AFM

Lucky Lady B-29 AFM

"Double Whammy" B-29 19 BG 12 AF NASM

Beaubomber II B-29 AFM

There'll Always Be A Christmas B-29 AFM

Snugglebunny B-29 44-69667 98 BG The original name was on the aircraft during its thirty-five missions in World War II. The artwork was added in Korea where it flew an additional sixty-five combat missions. *R. Mann*

Poison Ivy B-29 AFM

United Notions B-29 98 BG A play on words, United Nations, during the United Nations police action in Korea. *R. Mann*

"Deal Me In" B-29 44-96805 98 BG Original name was "Ace in the Hole;" changed by request of the chaplin. *R. Mann*

The Big Gass Bird B-29 98 BW Pronounced "Bigg Ass Bird." *AFM*

Mrs. Tittymouse B-29 42-65212 NASM

Chicago Sal B-29 AFM

Peace on Earth B-29 42-63412 AFM

Flak Maid B-29 44-70128 AFM

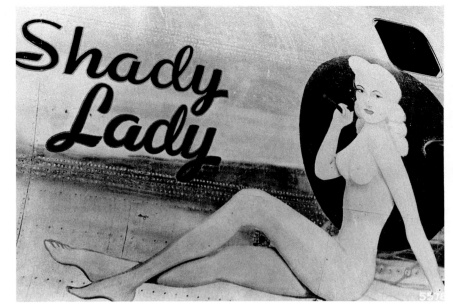

Shady Lady B-29 42-65357 98 BG AFM

Dragon Lady B-29 AFM

The Dragon Lady B-29 AFM

Wolf Pack B-29 44-86340 98 BG AFM

Our Baby B-29 42-24597 AFM

Little Gem B-29 AFM

184

Heavenly Laden B-29 44-61822 98 BG R. Mann

Cream of the Crop B-29 44-61657 19 BG 30 BS AFM

Four-A-Breast B-29 44-86323 19 BG 28 BS AFM

Beetle Bomb Er B-29 44-69800 98 BG Original artwork did not have the girl and was the "Beetle Bomb." AFM

Beetle Bomb B-29 J. Kolander

Purple Shaft B-29 AFM

Southern Comfort B-29 44-61749 19 BG 30 BS Lost over Korea November 1950. *AFM*

Our Gal B-29 19 BG *R. Mann*

The Uninvited B-29 Note the note. Must have been the last one in line during the last bombing run. *AFM*

The Wanderer B-29 44-62224 94 BG 325 BS Named for Lt. Col. Ralph Wanderer, commander of the 325th BS. So the story goes, Lt. Col. Wanderer was pushing for his full Col.'s bird when it came time to name this aircraft. The aircraft commander, Capt. B. Hemmingway, called it "The Wanderer." A close look reveals that those are not butterflys, but little eagles that he is chasing. *AFM*

Atomic Tom B-29 19 BG 93 BS *AFM*

Miss Megook B-29 "Gook" is slang for a Korean. *AFM*

186

The Wild Goose B-29 AFM

Loaded Dice B-29 AFM

Lucky Lady B-29 42-44863 AFM

Fire Belle B-29 AFM

Hump's Honey B-29 42-24648 AFM

Victory Girl B-29 42-24731 AFM

Dreamer B-29 J. Kolander

Mis-Chief-Mak-Er B-29 The girl is saying "I've had it before and want some more so come and get it. . . . Whos next!" AFM

Tail Wind B-29 J. Kolander

The Worry Bird B-29 Caption reads "Dis Ass Ter." J. Kolander

Liberty Belle B-29 92BG Painted by J. Kolander. J. Kolander

Peace on Earth B-29 J. Kolander

Downs' Clowns B-29 98 BG J. Kolander

Laggin Waggon B-29 44-65390 98 BG J. Kolander

Texas Doll B-29 AFM

Come on "A" My House B-29 AFM

Southern Belle B-29 42-63478 AFM

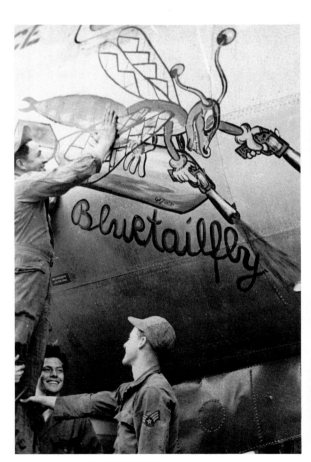

Bluetailfly B-29 NASM

Dauntless Dotty B-29 42-24382 NASM

Enola Gay B-29 The pilot, Col. Paul Tibbets, and the plane that dropped the first atomic bomb on (Hiroshima) Japan. The aircaft was named for his mother. Now in the process of restoration at the National Air and Space Museum. NASM

199

NOSE ART NAME	AIRCRAFT TYPE	PAGE NUMBER	NOSE ART NAME	AIRCRAFT TYPE	PAGE NUMBER	NOSE ART NAME	AIRCRAFT TYPE	PAGE NUMBER
Hotcha Baby	B-24	151	*Kipling's Error the III*	B-17	40	*Little Pedro*	B-17	41
"Hot" To Go	B-24	121	*Kiwi Boid*	A-26	168	*Little Pink Panties*	B-26	21
Hulcher's Vultures	B-17	54	*Knock-Out Dropper*	B-17	40	*Little Queen Mary*	B-24	151
Hump Happy Mammy	B-29	192	*Klap-Trap II, The*	B-17	40	*Little Red*	B-24	140
Hump's Honey	B-29	187	*Kongo Cutie*	C-87	122	*Little Tush*	B-17	41
Hump Time	B-24	82				*Lizzy Belle*	B-24	140
Hustlin' Hussy	B-17	39	*Lady Chance*	B-26	166	*Loaded Dice*	B-29	187
			Lady Godiva	B-26	165	*Loaded Leven*	B-29	176
Ice Cold Katy	B-17	39	*Lady Helen of Wimpole*	B-17	63	*Lonely Lady*	B-29	179
Ice Cold Katy	Jacket	75	*Lady in the Dark*	P-61	175	*Lonesome Lady*	B-24	122
Ice Col' Katy	B-17	39	*Lady Leone*	B-24	139	*Lonesome Polecat*	B-29	197
Idaliza	B-17	27	*Lady Luck*	B-24	85	*Lonesome Polecat Jr*	B-24	99
Idiots' Delight	B-17	98	*Lady Luck*	B-17	192	*Long Distance*	B-29	179
I'll Be Around	B-26	162	*Lady Mary Anna*	B-29	192	*Los Lobos*	B-17	41
I'll Be Seeing You	Jacket	75	*Lady Satan*	B-17	41	*Lou IV*	P-51	101
Impatient Virgin	B-17	62	*Laggin Dragon*	B-29	192	*Lovely Lisa*	Jacket	75
Impatient Virgin	B-17	62	*Laggin Waggon*	B-29	198	*Lucky Dog*	B-24	138
Incendiary Blonde	B-17	39	*Lakanooki*	B-24	139	*Lucky Lady*	B-29	181
Incendiary Blonde	B-25	155	*Lakanuki*	B-17	63	*Lucky Lady*	B-29	187
In Memory of Lt. F. Slanger USANC	P-38	171	*Lake Success Express*	B-29	190	*Lucky Lady*	B-29	193
Innocence A-Broad	B-24	138	*"Lassie", Come Home*	B-29	193	*Lucky Strike*	B-29	197
Innocent Infant	B-24	121	*Lassie I'm Home*	B-17	85	*Lucky Strike, The*	B-17	63
It Aint So Funny	B-24	121	*Late Date*	B-24	139	*Lucky Strike*	F-111	111
Iza Vailable Too	B-17	63	*Lay or Bust*	B-17	94	*Lucky Strike*	B-24	23
			Leo	B-24	90	*Luscious Lace*	B-24	122
Jack the Ripper	B-17	39	*Leroy's Joy*	B-25	155			
Jamaica?	B-24	20	*Lewd Angel*	B-17	41	*Madame Pele*	B-24	140
Jap-Happy	B-17	40	*Liberty Belle*	B-17	41	*Madame Queen*	Jacket	79
Jeeter Bug, The	B-24	148	*Liberty Belle*	B-29	198	*Madame Queen*	B-17	42
Jezebel	B-17	40	*Libra*	B-24	90	*Madame Shoo Shoo*	B-17	42
Jezebelle	B-24	121	*Lightning Strikes*	B-17	27	*Madame-X*	B-17	64
Jivin' Julie	B-25	161	*Lil Audrey*	B-24	139	*Mad Russian*	B-24	140
John Bull	B-26	163	*Lili Marlene*	B-24	123	*Mad Russian, The*	B-26	163
Joker, The	B-17	40	*Little Bit "O" Heav'n*	B-17	88	*Maggie*	B-17	43
Joker's Wild, The	B-17	71	*Little Buckaroo*	P-38	171	*Mairzy Doates*	B-24	96
Jokers Wild	B-29	177	*Little Cheezer*	Jacket	113	*Mama Lou*	A-20	169
Jungle Queen	B-24	121	*Little Chief*	?	173	*Mama Foo Foo*	B-24	12 & 83
Just Once More	B-17	81	*Little Flower*	B-24	121	*Manchester Misses*	B-17	43
Kansas City Kitty	B-24	122	*Little Gal*	B-26	165	*Man O War II*	B-17	61
Kansas Cyclone	B-24	138	*Little Gem*	B-29	184	*Margie*	B-17	44
Katie	B-29	192	*Little General, The*	B-24	139	*Margie Mae*	B-17	42
Kay Rashun	B-24	138	*Little Hiawatha*	B-24	139	*Marianna Ram*	B-29	193
Kickapoo-Kid	B-24	138	*Little Jo*	B-29	189	*Marlene*	B-24	123
King's X	B-24	122	*Little Miss Mischief*	B-17	99	*Marlin, The*	B-36	162
			Little Patches	B-17	63	*Mary Alice Gnatzi-Knight*	B-17	76
						Mary Cary	B-17	25
						Mary Lou	B-17	44
						Mary Loy	?	172

NOSE ART NAME	AIRCRAFT TYPE	PAGE NUMBER
Mask-A-Raid	B-24	151
Maximum Effort	B-17	64
Maytag Marauder	B-26	165
Meat Hound	B-17	42
Memphis Belle	B-17	65
Merry Boozer	B-24	140
Miami Clipper	B-17	64
Michigan	B-24	140
Mickey Mouse	B-17	71
Minnehaha	P-51	172
Minnie the Mermaid	B-17	44
Mis-Abortion	B-17	42
Mis Behavin	B-17	86
Mis-Chief-Mak-Er	B-29	189
Miss Barbara	B-17	94
Miss Bea Havin	B-17	26
Miss Bee Haven	B-24	141
Miss-Behav' in	B-25	156
Miss Beryl	B-24	124
Miss "B" Haven	B-17	20
Miss B Haven	Jacket	20
Miss Carriage	B-24	122
Miss Dee-Day	B-17	43
Miss Dorothy	B-24	123
Miss Fire	P-47	172
Miss Fit	B-24	18
Miss Gee Eyewanta (Go Home)	Jacket	20
Miss Hilda	B-24	124
Mission Belle	B-24	19 & 130
Mission Completed	B-17	84
Mission Inn	B-29	176
Miss Lace	B-17	44
Miss Lace	B-24	123
Miss Lace	B-29	193
Miss Laid	B-26	167
Miss Liberty	B-24	124
Miss Manchester	B-26	92
Miss Mass	P-38	172
Miss Megook	B-29	186
Miss Minooki	B-29	178
Miss N. C.	B-29	106
Miss Ouachita	B-17	64
Missouri Mule, The	B-24	141
Miss Patches	B-29	193
Miss Slip Stream	B-17	64
Miss Tennessee	B-24	124
Miss Traveler	B-24	154

NOSE ART NAME	AIRCRAFT TYPE	PAGE NUMBER
Miss Umbriago	B-17	43
Miss Wing Ding	Jacket	76
Miss Yourlovin	B-24	85
Mollita	B-17	43
Monkey Bizz-ness	B-17	64
Moose is Loose, The		24
Mors Ab Alto	B-24	83
Mrs. Tittymouse	B-29	183
Munda Belle	B-24	123
Murder Inc	B-26	163
Murphy's Mother in Law	B-24	141
Mustang, The	B-17	43
Mutz	?	86
Myakinas	B-29	197
Myasis Dragon	B-29	181
My Baby	B-17	65
My Bunnie II	B-24	141
My Diversion	B-24	141
Nana	B-24	125
Naturals	B-17	66
Near Miss	B-24	141
Nemesis of Aero-embolism	B-17	65
Never Hoppen	B-29	105
Next Objective	B-29	194
Nightmare	B-26	167
Night-mare	B-29	176
Night Mission	B-24	91
Night Mission	B-24	18
Nip-Pon-Ese	B-29	189
Nipponese Clipper	B-24	142
Nobby's Harriet J	B-17	12 & 86
Nocturnal Mission	B-24	152
Nora 2nd	B-17	65
No Sweat	B-29	106
Not in Stock	B-24	124
Not To-Day Cleo	B-17	44
Now Go!	B-17	44
Off We Go	B-24	154
Off We Go	Jacket	76
Ogoshi Ni	B-29	181
Oh Happy Day	B-17	45
Oh-7	B-25	98
Oklahoma Gal	B-24	142
Old Bill	B-17	45
Old Coffins	B-17	45
Old Crow	?	163

NOSE ART NAME	AIRCRAFT TYPE	PAGE NUMBER
Old Glory	B-17	66
Old Irongut	B-17	24
Old Rusty	P-38	93
Ole Baldy	B-24	92
Ole' Swayback	B-17	45
Ol' Mac	B-17	45
O-O-Nothing	B-24	91
Oooold Soljer	B-17	45
Ou-La-La	A-20	160
Our Baby	B-26	163
Our Baby	B-29	184
Our Boarding House	B-17	46
Our Bridget	B-17	66
Our Gal	B-29	103
Our Gal	B-29	186
Our Gal	B-29	181
Our Gal	B-24	21
Our Gal Ardelle	B-25	155
Our Gal Sal	B-17	94
Out House Mouse	B-17	66
Out of This World	B-24	142
Over Exposed	?	19
Over Exposed!	B-29	194
Over Exposed	B-24	152
Pachyderm	B-24	154
Pacific Passion	B-24	126
Pacific Tramp III	B-24	125
Pakawalup	B-17	46
Pappy	L-3	100
Pappy's Passion	B-24	126
Passion Wagon	B-29	180
Patched Up Piece	B-24	126
Patches n' Prayers	B-17	25
Patent Pending	Jacket	76
Patty Jo	B-17	46
Peace Maker	B-29	95
Peacemaker, The	B-17	66
Peace Offering	B-24	152
Peace on Earth	B-29	183
Peace on Earth	B-29	198
Peace or Bust	B-17	46
Pelican, The	B-24	150
Pella Tulip	B-17	46
Perpetual Help	B-17	66
Peter Heater, The	B-24	126
Philbert 3	P-38	172
Phippen's Pippins	B-29	177

NOSE ART NAME	AIRCRAFT TYPE	PAGE NUMBER
Photo Fanny	B-24	125
Photo Queen	B-24	142
Piccadilly Lilly II	B-27	67
Pink's Lady II	B-26	168
Pistol Packin' Mama	B-17	46
Pistol Packin' Mama	Jackets	72
Pistol Packing Mama	B-24	125
Pistol Pakin Mamma	B-24	142
Play Boy	B-24	142
Pleasure Bent	B-24	143
Plunderbus	B-24	143
Pluto	B-25	158
Poison Ivy	B-29	182
Ponderous Peg	B-29	194
Poopsie	B-25	161
Pregnant Portia	B-17	47
Posse	P-38	172
Potch-a-Galoop	B-25	158
Pride of the "Kiarians"	B-17	47
Pride of the Yankees	B-25	160
Prince Charming	B-24	115
Princess Eileen II	B-29	196
Princess Konocti	B-24	125
Problem Child	B-25	155
Prop Wash	B-25	155
Prop Wash	Jacket	76
Punched Fowl, The	B-17	47
Purple Shaft	B-29	185
Purrin Panther	B-26	165
Queenie	B-17	67
Queen Mae	B-24	126
Queen of Hearts	B-24	108
Queen of the Neches	B-29	196
Queen Sally	Jacket	76
Raging Red	B-17	67
Ramp Queen	B-29	180
Ramp Rooster	B-17	47
Rangy Lil	B-24	152
Rationed Passion	B-26	164
Rat Poison	B-17	47
Raz'n Hell	B-29	106
Ready 4 Duty	C-47	109

NOSE ART NAME	AIRCRAFT TYPE	PAGE NUMBER
Ready Willing and Able	B-24	127
Rebel's Revenge	B-17	67
Red Butt	B-24	126
Red Gremlin, The	B-17	67
Red Hot Riding Hood	?	175
Redmond Annie	B-17	47
Redwing	B-17	68
Riot Call	B-24	143
Rip Snorter	B-24	127
Rock Happy	B-29	176
Rose O' Day	B-24	152
Rose of Juarez	B-24	143
Rosie's Sweat Box	Jacket	77
Rough-Neck	B-17	48
Roxy's Special	B-17	48
Royal Flush!	B-17	68
Ruby's Raiders	B-17	68
Ruff Knights	B-24	143
Rum Buggy	B-26	168
Rum+Coke	B-17	88
Rusty Dusty	B-17	48
Ruthless Ruthie	B-24	143
Sack Time	B-17	48
Sack Time	B-24	91
Sack Time	B-17	48
Sack Time Sal II	B-24	144
Sad Sack, The	B-25	158
Sagittarius	B-24	14
Saint & Ten Sinners, The	B-17	48
Sal	B-25	157
Salem's Angel	Jacket	112
Salty Sal	B-24	144
Salvo Sadie	Jacket	18
Salvo Sadie	B-17	17
San Antonio Rose	?	174
Satan's Baby	B-24	128
Satan's Sister	B-26	164
Scarlett O'Hara	B-17	72
Scheherazade	B-17	68
Schnozzle	B-17	100
Scorchy II	B-17	49
Scorpion	B-26	166
Scrapiron IV	P-38	175
Scrappy Jr	B-17	26
Screamin' Demon	B-17	78
Screamin' Red Ass	B-17	49
Screw	B-17	49

NOSE ART NAME	AIRCRAFT TYPE	PAGE NUMBER
Screwball Express	B-17	26
Scrumptious	B-26	19
Secrut Weapin	B-24	144
Senta A Pua	?	96
Sentimental Journey	B-17	110
Sentimental Journey	B-29	188
Settin Pretty	B-24	128
Sexy Sue II	B-24	149
Shack, The	B-24	24 & 112
Shack Bunny	B-17	49
Shackeroo! II	B-17	68
Shack-Rabbit	B-17	24
Shade Ruff	B-17	77
Shady Lady	B-24	94
Shady Lady	B-24	144
Shady Lady	B-29	184
Shady Lady	B-29	196
Shanghai Lil Rides Again	B-29	181
Shangri-La-Lil	B-17	49
Shedonwanna?	B-17	68
Sheeza Goer!	B-29	194
Sheriff's Posse	B-17	61
She's A Honey	B-17	49
Shoo Shoo Baby	B-17	25
Shoo Shoo Baby	B-17	50
Shoo-Shoo Baby	B-24	50
Short Run!	B-24	128
Shy Ann	B-24	152
Sit n Git	B-26	69
Sitting Pretty	B-24	127
Skonk Works	A-20	169
Skunk Hunter	B-25	158
Sky Cowboy	P-38	173
Skyhag	B-26	167
Slammin' Spammy	B-24	127
Slave Girl	B-29	188
Sleepy	B-24	115
Sleepy Time Gal	B-17	18
Sleepy Time Gal	B-24	84
Sleepy Time Gal	B-26	18
Slick Chick	Jacket	80
Slightly Dangerous	B-17	50
Sloppy But Safe	B-24	12 & 82
Sluggin' Sal	B-24	127
Smashing Time	B-17	50
Smokey Stover	B-24	144
Snake Bit	B-29	196
Snap! Crackle! Pop!	B-17	69
Sneezy	B-24	115